Endorsements

This book is filled with telling insight from a seasoned pastor's wife who has seen the pitfalls of immodesty. It is more than a call to cover; it is a cry to return to holiness and the modeling of Christ in every aspect of your life.

—Lisa Bevere, Author/Speaker
Kissed the Girls and Made Them Cry

As a 35-year veteran in full-time youth ministry, I'm cheering wildly for *What Guys See That Girls Don't...Or Do They?* Sharon has dared to discuss issues that are both sensitive and life-changing. My years in youth ministry allow me to boldly affirm that these principles are far from legalistic—but liberating and destiny-filled. I join with the angels who are saying, "Go, Sharon, go!"

—Jeanne Mayo, President
Youth Source Mentoring Resources

I challenge every teenage girl and every female Christian leader to read this book and allow the Holy Spirit to deal a deathly blow to the lies that this world tries to sell us through media, fashion design, and the porn industry. Sharon will convince and teach you how to live a life of purity in a culture that no longer values modesty and how to reclaim the blessing and power of God in your life.

—Katie Luce
Teen Mania Ministries

What
Guys see
that girls
Don't...
or do they?

What
Guys see
that girls
Don't...
or do they?

Sharon Daugherty

Destiny Image® Publishers, Inc.
P.O. Box 310
Shippensburg, PA 17257-0310

"Speaking to the Purposes of God for this Generation
and for the Generations to Come."

For Worldwide Distribution, Printed in the U.S.A.

ISBN 10: 0-7684-2368-6
ISBN 13: 978-0-7684-2368-6

This book and all other Destiny Image, Revival Press, MercyPlace, Fresh Bread, Destiny Image Fiction, and Treasure House books are available at Christian bookstores and distributors worldwide.

1 2 3 4 5 6 7 8 9 10 11 / 09 08 07 06

For a U.S. bookstore nearest you, call
1-800-722-6774.

For more information on foreign distributors, call
717-532-3040.

Or reach us on the Internet:
www.destinyimage.com

Contents

Somebody Is Watching You

L IKE it or not, you're being watched. People watch people. Guys particularly watch girls and women. They watch how you dress. They watch your behavior patterns. They watch any signals you send. Whether you are naive or purposeful in what you do makes no difference to the fact that they watch you. They are aware of both circumstances—they do recognize naiveness, and they know when a girl is purposefully luring them.

Girls who are fashion conscious but naive to the fact that society is pushing sexual freedom and hedonism (the attitude of "whatever feels good, do it") could be setting themselves up for hurt and regret.

I remember a young, beautiful Christian woman who always dressed in the latest fashion, wearing clothes tight enough and open enough to emphasize her good figure. She simply thought people would admire her good figure, assuming that guys would just "look but not touch." She liked being watched, but was not prepared for someone crossing the boundary with her. She didn't realize that there was a guy watching her and waiting for the moment to rape her. Of course, he had no right to rape her—but did she set herself up? She was a Christian who had grown up in church and had always felt very protected.

How far does God's protection go when we move beyond the boundaries that God's Word and His Holy Spirit have warned us to establish? Is it possible for a Christian girl or woman to believe in God, attend church regularly, have a daily devotion time, but go beyond the boundary of "the secret place" of God's covering (see Ps. 91) and become an open target for attack?

Some girls don't want to think about it. They want to believe that as long as they aren't thinking about sexually arousing a guy, even if they are dressing immodestly or wearing clothes that focus on certain body parts, they are okay.

Many times girls just don't realize that what they wear or how they carry themselves send signals to guys. Hosea 4:6 says, "[God's] *people are destroyed for lack of knowledge....*" Where there is a lack of knowledge, there is a lack of discernment and discretion, which will lead a girl or woman into trouble. And the enemy (satan) is always looking for an opportunity of trouble (see 1 Pet 5:8.) On the other hand, there are girls and women who are *not* naive in the way they dress; they purposefully take a risk for trouble because of a need for attention.

In either case, this book is to help you examine your life and find God's will regarding how you relate to others in your dress, behavior, and lifestyle. God wants to keep you and protect you as you live within the boundaries of His secret place.

—Sharon Daugherty

Chapter One

Is Modesty in Style at All?

WHAT does it mean to be "in style"? Style is the prevailing fashion trend at a particular time. To be "in style" is to do and wear what everyone else seems to be doing and wearing. If we look around right now, I think we all can see that modesty doesn't appear to be "in style." It definitely is not the prevailing fashion trend. Wherever you go in public, whenever you turn on the TV, you are faced with lots of skin and "in your face" bodies of girls and women.

Fashion designers promote clothes that reveal as much skin as possible, while still leaving a few threads on the body. Choosing to advertise this type of clothing reveals that they live in a darkened understanding (see Rom. 1:21). Without a God consciousness, there is no moral compass or guide. And when designers design clothes without a moral guide, they have no sense of responsibility for the society of people for whom they are making clothes; consequently, they will design and market a product to the absolute limits that the public will accept. What's on their minds is creating something new and different in order to entice people to buy their fashions. Everything is subject to change, and they continue to change fashion so that people will continue to buy and spend money, so that they can keep making money.

Modesty may not be something that clothing designers are considering right at the moment, but that could change—all things are possible. One thing is for sure—there is a great Designer who is thinking about modesty—the "Master Fashion Designer"—God Himself. Would you like to know exactly what He thinks? He wrote His will to Christians in First Timothy 2:9: "*I would like for women to wear modest and sensible clothes...*" (CEV). There you go! That's pretty plain and understandable. It's amazing that there was a need to address this issue of women's clothes even then. God obviously knew that hundreds and thousands of years later, we would need this instruction as well.

An interesting fact is that this Book of the Bible was written from an older single man named Paul to a young single pastor named Timothy, instructing him to tell the girls and women at his church to dress modestly.

Today, more than ever before, modesty needs to be addressed among Christian girls and women who go to church week after week. Pastors, youth pastors, and men who attend church are speaking up and saying, "Please put some clothes on that cover your body and don't emphasize your body parts. Dress so that guys don't have to deal with thoughts of lust when they go to church." Church should be considered a "safe house," not a house of seduction.

Modesty—An Issue of the Law or a Matter of the Heart?

In an article from *The Nebraska Civic Digest Newspaper*, June 2003, "Why Do Nice Girls Dress Like That?" by Joanne Brokaw, an interview was held with "Out of Eden," a Christian rhythm and blues hip-hop group. One of the singers, Andrea Baca, thinks that girls are copying what they see in the media, and as a result, they don't see a problem showing skin. "I definitely think our culture infiltrates our young people with the message that the most important thing is how you look, how you are showing, or how sexy you are." She points out that some Christian artists aren't helping. "You see people who are Christians who have gone into the mainstream even changing the idea of what's modest because it fits our culture. So obviously, young girls are going to say, 'I guess it's okay,' or, 'I guess it's what I have to do in order to be accepted.'"

So how far do we go to be accepted? And does our desire for acceptance in this world's culture exceed our need for acceptance by God? Does it matter to God? Does God have anything to say about modesty? Is modesty a requirement for Christians?

There are many different views and opinions on modesty. Some consider it an outdated word and do not even give it a thought. Others have never heard anyone actually explain it so they can understand it.

Years ago, "modesty" was an accepted and understood characteristic of being a Christian. There was a differentiation of the dress, behavior, and lifestyle of Christians from those who were not saved. This differentiation revealed that Christians desired to live a holy, separated, devoted life committed to Jesus. There was a realization that what a person wore could have a negative or a positive effect upon other people.

Over the years, some Christians took modesty into a strict, legalistic direction as a law instead of a motivation of love, which caused others to "buck against" and gradually lose sight of its purpose.

Let me say that modesty is not about legalism or just keeping laws. *Modesty is a matter of the heart and an attitude of surrender to Jesus' lordship*. God always starts with the heart of a person. If He has our heart, then He has the ability to mold us and direct us in the right direction that is godly, because He is godly. If modesty isn't understood from the position of a surrendered heart, a person will see it as legalism or law, and he or she will probably at some point rebel against it and say, "I can't do it." They don't want to make the effort to do it because their will hasn't become surrendered and submitted. They still want freedom to do whatever they want to do or what circumstances around them are tempting them to do.

Some Christians, in trying to relate with the world around them, have felt they should look more like the world. Let me just say that winning people to Jesus is not about looking like the unsaved or doing exactly what they do. I don't have to take drugs to minister to a drug addict, or become a prostitute, or even look like a prostitute, in order to relate and minister to her. What they want to know is that I sincerely love and care for them and that I know how they can be set free.

Many Christians have become squeezed into the mold of this world's views and have totally lost a *holy* perspective in living their lives as a light in the middle of this world's darkness. God needs Christians to be Christians, which can happen only if we are surrendered to Jesus and if we keep ourselves in that surrendered and submitted attitude with Him on a daily basis. After I surrendered my life to Jesus and grew in my walk with Him, I became aware of God's holy desire in the way I lived and even in the way I dressed.

I remember during one semester in college, I roomed with a girl who had been raised in a very strict home and a legalistic church background. Because she had never experienced a point of surrender in her life, she saw her Christian life as rules and regulations. So, once she was away from home, she felt free to break her parents' rules and go beyond their boundaries. She made sure that she abided—just barely—to the school rules, and she pushed everything as far as she could. Because we attended a Christian university, we were subjected to certain guidelines and boundaries, but this did not stop her from living on the edge of those boundaries. And because she had some extra money, she bought the clothes she wasn't allowed to buy at home. Even though we were different from one another, we had a good relationship for the short time we roomed together. Our conversations helped me to see a realm of Christianity that I had not experienced before. I saw the effects of legalism with no love. (I found it interesting that the liberal denomination I had come from had actually frustrated me and driven me to desire God's standards of modesty and a consecrated lifestyle.) It appeared that her church background had somehow missed showing her that "surrender" of her heart would mean that she would want to please God in the way she lived and dressed, and that's what modesty has to be based on.

I believe that in many great moves of God, from which many churches have originated, people experienced total surrender and made the effort to honor God with their lives. However, as years have passed, some parents and church denominations, in an effort to point the next generation in a godly direction, have passed down strict biblical laws and boundaries for their children to live by without passing down the understanding of *surrender* to Jesus and *love* for Him. This most important part teaches that *real love always produces the fruit of wanting to please the one whom you love.*

Eventually, some of the next generation of these church denominations or people groups who had never learned about a love relationship with God rebelled and began to break away from the laws, even leaving those particular churches. This was the case for my roommate.

Christians can be like the pendulum of a clock. They can swing to the one side—a liberal, no-commitment mind-set, or they can head the opposite direction—a strict, legalistic, unloving mind-set. In either case, love can cause the pendulum of the clock to function correctly. *When we love God more than this world's way of thinking and we love other people from God's perspective, we'll do the right thing.* The law of love will guide us to please God above anyone else, and to love others because we don't want to cause them any vulnerability of stumbling in their Christian walk.

Throughout history, the standards of modesty have varied with each generation and culture of people of the time; but *even though clothing trends have changed, modesty is still a very integral part of living a devoted life to Jesus.* The nature of Jesus is holy and pure, and when He comes into a person's life and establishes His rule, His Holy Spirit begins to bring every area of a person's life into a holy and pure direction.

Surrendering to Jesus' lordship will begin to change everything in your life—the words you speak, the clothes you wear, the music you listen to, the movies you watch, the places you go, and the habits you develop. The Holy Spirit will convict and convince you of what is not right in order to make things right (see John 16:8). He writes God's laws in our minds and our hearts (see Heb. 8:10). He speaks to us (see Heb. 12:25, 3:7-10; John 16:13), and His written Word corrects us as well.

Our Clothes Communicate

The attitude of compromise has affected many Christians and churches today, and even some in leadership positions have compromised their lifestyles. Other leaders have been afraid to speak up and bring attention to areas that need to be corrected because of fear of offending people. Sometimes in the desire to be accepted and popular, a person agrees with the crowd to please them instead of standing up to and challenging them toward what is right. It takes strength to go against the crowd and *lovingly* speak up and *address what needs to be corrected.* I personally have come to realize that it is good for each of us to check ourselves regularly, making sure we are seeking to please Jesus and not simply conforming to the world's standards or what other Christians' ideas may be, which are not godly.

In an article in *Charisma* magazine, August 2004, titled, "Put on Some Clothes!" Valerie Lowe shared, "Last year when a well-known female preacher arrived at a Pentecostal conference wearing an extremely tight dress, leaders of the group apologized to attendees and promised, 'She will never preach here again.'"

Do you think that was harsh? Let me ask you another question: Do you think she was dressing to please God or to just look good? I don't know who this person is, but if she wasn't convicted over the situation, it is possible that her heart has become hardened to that still small voice. The more sensitive we are to His still small voice, the more sensitive we will be in how we come across to those we desire to reach or teach. Romans 14:15 indicates that when your brother (or sister) in Christ is grieved over what you are doing, it's time to evaluate your love walk. It's time to consider how much you are willing to lay down in order to communicate the Gospel of Jesus.

In this article, Valerie Lowe continues: "One Florida pastor, frustrated about immodest dress among his congregants, confronted the problem during Sunday morning worship. 'When you wear your clothes tight and too short, you're making a statement about yourself. My advice to you is, "If you are not for sale, please take the sign down!"'"

Here is another question: What kind of girls or women sell themselves? Here's an answer: The kind who make money with their bodies. Is that the kind of woman you want others to view you as? Is there such a thing as a Christian prostitute? According to God's Word, the answer to that question is "No." (I realize in our society's mind-set today, some might have different opinions. However, our standard to live by is not the opinions of others but the opinion of God.)

Does the grace of God remove self-restraint and consideration for others? It seems that many in the church world have focused so much on a "no boundary" grace and freedom that they have removed any sense of responsibility of restraint on themselves. Self-restraint and consideration of others are characteristics of being led by the Holy Spirit. Having boundaries in our lives is fruit of true Christianity. Remember, one fruit of the Spirit is self-control (see Gal. 5:22-23).

Today it can be hard to tell if a girl is a Christian or not if you only take into account the way she dresses. Most girls dress according to fashion without thinking about it. But whether you realize it or not, you are communicating to others with your clothes.

This may be a new thought for you to consider. We not only communicate with our words, but we communicate with how we dress. For example, it's a general understanding that if an event you are attending is casual, you might wear clothes such as jeans and a T-shirt. If you were to wear a formal evening gown at this function, people would look at you strangely. Whereas, if you attended a more formal occasion, you would probably wear a formal dress or a semi-formal pantsuit. Anything casual would draw attention as being "out of place." The type of gathering you are attending is communicated by what you wear.

Here's another thought to consider: *We also communicate by the way we wear our clothes.* We communicate if we are secure or insecure, in need of attention, or fearful of any attention, seductive, deceptive, guarded or loose, feminine or manly, naive or totally aware. In any case, no matter what the occasion, or what we are wearing, or how we are wearing it, the Word of God tells us God's will is for us to dress modestly. And so, let's look at what modesty really means.

Modesty—A Sense of Restraint

Webster defines *modesty* as being "properly restrained by a sense of propriety (or having a moral law that a person conforms to); not loose or lewd; having chastity."[1] (Note: We would say not being forward or bold is not being seductive or flirtatious.) The word *lewd* in this definition means "intending to excite lust or sexual desire."[2] Also in the definition above is the word *chastity*, which is an old English word that means "being pure; having an innocence; the absence of seductive influence; abstaining from acts or thoughts that do not agree with virginity or strict marital fidelity; not indulging in sexual activity or encouraging it."[3]

If Noah Webster were alive today, he would probably be shocked at how women currently dress. He might even think that girls and women everywhere were prostitutes. He would possibly stay inside his house so that he would not be tempted to lose his fidelity or purity by what he saw all around him.

Stop and think how much our society has changed and how it exposes all parts of the female body as normal, accepted fashion. When you look at what Christian girls wear today as well, it appears that limitations are no longer regarded.

When Paul wrote his letter to young Timothy, he said that he needed to tell girls and women to dress "modestly" and "sensibly." Another version says "with soberness" (ABUV). The word "sensibly" is actually the Greek word *sophrosune*. *Sophrosune* means "to place a voluntary limitation on one's freedom of thought and behavior." The *Conybeare Translation* says, "with self-restraint." Our freedom in Christ is not about removing what we consider to be limitations that actually produce a godly lifestyle. It's about being free from satan's power to influence our lives. Once we accept Jesus' lordship, He convicts us to place restraint upon our lifestyle in order to honor God. Today, our society would probably disdain and criticize Noah Webster, Paul, Timothy, and other great men in history for their strict moral way of thinking; but in centuries past, modesty was an accepted virtue in society, because our whole society was influenced by Christianity and Judaism. which are both based upon living according to the standards of the Bible. Immodesty symbolized prostitution.

In the *Charisma* article by Valerie Lowe, John Stossel of ABC's 20/20 is quoted as saying that since fashion designers are now creating "sexy" clothes for little children as well as for teens and adults, what will they design for prostitutes? How far has our society gone? And how far will you as a Christian go in order to look like a society that has lost restraint?

Thoughts to Remember

Here are some closing thoughts to remember:

1. The "Master Fashion Designer"—God Himself—wrote His will regarding modesty in First Timothy 2:9: "*I would like for women to wear modest and sensible clothes...*" (CEV).

2. What you wear, as well as how you wear your clothes, communicates a message. The way you dress can have a negative or a positive effect upon other people.

3. Modesty is not about legalism. It's a matter of the heart and an attitude of surrender to Jesus' lordship.

4. In dressing "sensibly," we understand that the original meaning of this word *sophrosune* is to place a voluntary limitation on one's freedom of thought and behavior. Another translation says "with self-restraint." Our freedom in Christ is not about removing what we consider to be limitations that actually produce a godly lifestyle. It's about being free from satan's power to influence our lives.

5. Even though clothing trends have changed, modesty is still a very integral part of living a devoted life to Jesus.

6. Real love always produces the fruit of wanting to please the one you love. We should regularly evaluate our love life toward Jesus and others.

7. Modesty is a decision that goes against the tide of popular opinion. It is a choice to honor Jesus Christ in your everyday life, and that includes what you wear.

Endnotes

1. Noah Webster, *1828 American Dictionary of the English Language*, Foundation for American Christian Education, San Francisco, California.

2. *Webster's New World College Dictionary* (New York, NY: A Simon & Schuster Macmillan Co., 1997), 777.

3. Noah Webster, *1828 American Dictionary of the English Language*.

Chapter Two

What Caused
Our Society to Change?

L OOKING back on history, I believe that *humanism* can be credited for changing the moral fabric of our society. At the turn of the 20th century, humanism began to replace Christian concepts in our public educational system, ethics began to fade, and a worldly view became more widely accepted. Humanism exalts man's opinions above God's. In fact, humanists do not believe there is a God, nor do they believe the Bible is absolute truth or that there even are any absolutes. (By the way, if you believe the Bible, you are considered by humanists to be an "absolutist.")

With regard to the philosophy of humanism, man becomes his own god and decides what is right or wrong according to the situation he finds himself in. It's called situational ethics. Humanists do not believe in set moral absolutes like the Ten Commandments. There are no absolutes regarding right and wrong, no set boundaries morally or ethically. Each person makes his own determination at the moment of his or her situation and environment, and according to his or her desires or lust. (Note: This helps you understand why some have wanted to remove the Ten Commandments from public places. They do not want any reminder of restraint on their passions and lusts.) Humanists believe that all beliefs and all lifestyles are equal. What is reality to one person may be different from another person's reality, and according to humanists, neither is wrong.

The Cost of Humanism

I remember once talking to a lady in our church whose husband had left her for another woman. Because he continued to stay in the sexual relationship with the other woman, he quit attending our church, and he and the other woman started attending another church together where no one knew them.

His wife asked him if he and the other woman felt any conviction about living together, though unmarried, when they attended church. He replied that he didn't have any remorse for what he was doing. He told her that what was wrong to her (his wife) did not make it wrong to him. He went on to say that each person has the right to determine for himself what is right or wrong and that there is no absolute right or wrong. Each person determines his or her own moral direction.

His wife was shocked at his response and his belief. She said she had not realized how he had been affected by the humanistic mind-set. Before they were married, he had claimed to be a Christian and attended a strong church for a few years, but obviously he had not surrendered and submitted his beliefs to the lordship of Jesus Christ. He became swayed by the mind-set of our society's humanistic belief. Fortunately, by an act of God's intervention, this man came back to his wife a year later with great remorse and repentance asking her forgiveness for his deception and the hurt he had caused her.

Are you aware of the poisonous mixture that has seeped into many Christians' lives who have been influenced by the media and by public education? Realizing the times we are living in and choosing to obey God's Word rather than live by the mind-set of our society could determine whether or not you will have a marriage that stands against storms or is destroyed by them. In eternity it could mean whether or not a person enters Heaven or hell.

Galatians 5:19-21 lists the lusts of the flesh and says that those (and Paul was writing to Christians) who *do* such things will not inherit the Kingdom of God. The word "do" in the Greek means to make something a practice or to keep doing something—where their actions become the norm and their pattern of life. God says in His Word that if you keep *doing* a sin that you know is wrong and you do not make an effort to repent of it, deny it, stop doing it, and avoid it, you will not inherit the Kingdom of God.

The Spread of Humanism and Evolution

In the early part of the 20th century, humanism was introduced in the educational process to challenge the thinking of a nation of people who had been rooted and established in a biblical worldview. As years passed, humanism began to replace the Judeo Christian mind-set in public education, removing belief in God and the influence of the Bible from daily education. This created a mind-set of no boundaries and removed a sense of conscience regarding right and wrong.

It was during the 1960s then, that one woman cunningly deceived our nation to remove prayer and Bible reading from all public schools. Without these moral compasses daily available in the lives of children, our society experienced a drastic change in every way. Humanism and evolution had already wormed their way into the higher levels of education in our universities. (Did you know that many of these universities had at one time been Christian, such as Yale, Princeton, Dartmouth, and Harvard?) Now humanism was able to spread like an unattended wildfire throughout grade schools across the country, affecting the minds of all children—children who would become adults who would govern the nation. (Refer to Fritz Ridenour's book, *So What's the Difference?*)

I remember talking to a woman from the former Soviet Union who shared with me that when communism ruled there, humanism and evolution were the belief systems that the communists promoted. They told the people there was no God, the Bible was not true, and there were no moral absolutes. She said that the people began to feel that there was nothing wrong with sex outside of marriage and there was nothing wrong with having an abortion. It became an accepted form of contraception. She said most men thought there was nothing wrong with having a wife and a mistress at the same time. It was common for most men to drink vodka daily after work; consequently, when they came home, they were abusive toward their family. Integrity was no longer a value to their society, and lying became common, especially if it benefited them personally. Without a God-consciousness, deception ran rampant. In addition, there were many cruelties that transpired during the years of communist rule in the Soviet Union.

Communism embraced humanism and evolution because these beliefs removed moral restraints and promoted the lies that there is no God and that the Bible is not true. Proponents of evolution believe that "human beings did not fall from perfection into sin as the church has taught for centuries, we were evolving, and indeed are still evolving, into higher levels of consciousness."[1] These proponents do not want to believe in sin or the need to repent of sin. They believe that "survival of the fittest" does away with moral values based on divine law. Man determines for himself what is right for the moment. If he thinks he needs to get rid of another man, he decides what he thinks needs to be done. Evolution believes there is nothing special or sacred about humanity. Instead, it reduces man to a highly developed animal who is no more valuable than a cow or a chicken. Evolution also believes that there is no purpose or meaning to life. (This is why some have no problem in taking someone's life if people are no more valuable than animals.)

Now, after considering what humanism and evolution are determined to destroy, realize that these beliefs are being taught in every public school and university in America. Indeed, many schools have rejected the creationist belief to the point that they allow only evolution to be taught. They attempt to claim that creationism is a religious belief, whereas evolution is not. The fact is, humanism and evolution are just as much religious beliefs as creationism. Evolution simply allows those teaching it to say and do whatever they want. Creationism establishes boundaries. In addition, the humanist and evolutionist mind-sets can also be credited for the legalization of abortion in our country and the loss of many other moral boundaries that we once had. (For more information, see the book, *So What's the Difference?* by Fritz Ridenour.)

Are Values and Restraint Things of the Past?

Recently, in an Oklahoma newspaper, an article was written titled "Whose Values?" which said, "If polls are to be believed, there is no one set of traditional American values any more, if there ever was. The traditional, nuclear American family, along with its accompanying values, has become an elusive species, and taking its place is a new animal."[2]

Notice, there is a doubt placed in the reader's mind regarding if there ever was any traditional American values. Let me reiterate that America's founding fathers established our nation "under God" and used the Bible as a guide in writing our Constitution and in setting moral values, even in the required books read by students in schools across America. Sadly, many changes have taken place since that time.

When a society rejects God and the Bible, it will eventually destroy itself unless it reawakens itself to God. The Bible gives a society a standard of morality and ethics based upon love and respect for God and mankind that prevents people from destroying themselves and others if they will accept that standard and live by it. The Bible also says, "*The fool hath said in his heart, There is no God....*" (Ps. 14:1). Humanists and evolutionists say this very thing, and God calls them fools, who have a wicked motive behind their godless beliefs.

Aldous Huxley, an influential writer on the theory of evolution said:

> I had motive for not wanting the world to have a meaning; consequently assumed that it had none, and was able without any difficulty to find satisfying reasons for this assumption. *The philosopher who finds no meaning in the world* is not concerned exclusively with a problem in pure metaphysics, *he is also concerned to prove that there is no valid reason why he personally should not do as he wants to do, or why his friends should not seize political power and govern in the way that they find most advantageous to themselves....For myself, the philosophy of meaninglessness was essentially an instrument of liberation, sexual and political.*[3]

> The philosopher who finds no meaning in the world is not concerned exclusively with a problem in pure metaphysics; he is also concerned to prove that there is no valid reason why he personally should not do as he wants to do....For myself, as, no doubt, for most of my contemporaries, the philosophy of meaninglessness was essentially an instrument of liberation. *The liberation we desired was simultaneously liberation...from a certain*

system of morality. We objected to the morality because it interfered with our sexual freedom; we objected to the political and economic system because it was unjust. The supporters of these systems claimed that in some way they embodied the meaning (a Christian meaning), they insisted of the world. There was one admirably simple method of confuting these people and at the same time justifying ourselves in our political and erotic revolt; we could deny that the world had any meaning whatsoever.[4]

David King Dunaway was quoted in "Huxley in Hollywood" (Harper & Row) as saying:

Aldous and [his wife] Maria had what now would be regarded as an open marriage, with Maria's going so far as to arrange liaisons for her husband with other women. Bedford explained Maria's liberalism in terms of an "aristocratic view of sex." Dunaway discovered through conversations with Maria's family that she was a lesbian and that she and Aldous shared an appreciation for beautiful women. Working from this new perspective on the Huxleys' marital arrangement, Dunaway proceeds to place Maria within the Hollywood 'Sewing Circles'—the underground lesbian community that included women such as Mercedes De Acosta, Greta Garbo's companion. He suggests that Maria particularly enjoyed the swinging Hollywood lifestyle during the thirties; and to indicate something of the milieu of the times, he takes a side trip or two to look at the Hollywood homosexual community, which apparently included not only famous film stars but also two of Huxley's best friends....[5]

Many Christians have no clue of the underlying motive of humanism and evolution teaching, which is to "cast off all restraint" in order to live by one's lust. However, Psalm 2:3 says of those who do not want to believe in God and do not want to listen to the people of God, "*Let us break their bands asunder* [the Hebrew word is *mocerah*, to cast off restraint], *and cast away their cords from us* [the Hebrew word is *aboth*, meaning ropes or whatever is holding them]."[6] There are people who desire to do whatever they want to do without feeling any remorse. Yet when a person rejects the convicting voice of the Holy Spirit and continues to do wrong, God's Word says that condemnation will be the result. If a person repents, that condemnation will vanish. However, if the person does not repent, his or her own heart can become hardened to the point that they no longer accept fault or guilt for wrongdoing.

John 3:19-20 says:

And this is the condemnation, that light is come into the world, and men loved darkness rather than light, because their deeds were evil. For every one that doeth evil hateth the light, neither cometh to the light, lest his deeds should be reproved [corrected].

Those who accept the Holy Spirit's conviction and correction reveal that they love the light and love Jesus more than the darkness and the wrong they have been committing.

The world system continues to reject moral restraint, and the media constantly bombards people to accept a liberal view of "no moral absolutes." Television sitcoms, talk show interviews, movies, and even the news networks encourage freedom of boundaries, openness to sex with many people in order to discover the right one, lying, compromising in order to gain position, and getting rid of any sense of guilt for fulfilling your own lust.

The thought that every human should decide for himself if he wants to live morally or not continues to spread. Of course, this way of thinking releases a person from feeling any *responsi-*

bility in causing others to stumble or in hurting others while exercising their own freedom of choice. And even more devastating, the result of the world's changing view of morality and self-restraint has penetrated into the church. Although some Christians have continued to maintain boundaries, many have given over to a compromising view, not wanting to be different than the world so that the world will accept them.

When someone believes in moral absolutes, self restraint and consideration of others will not be difficult to accept as part of living the Christian life.

For Christians, modesty is a decision that goes against the tide of popular opinion. It's a choice to honor Jesus Christ in our everyday life. *And yes, you can still dress stylish while establishing some restraints upon the way you wear your clothes.* It's not about legalistic views; it is about living in surrender to Jesus and being submitted to the voice of the Holy Spirit. Some people think that the Holy Spirit operates in them only at church or just when a person needs some extra guidance. The Holy Spirit lives within Christians to guide us every day in God's directions, in His views, and in His way of thinking. His ways and His thoughts are better than our ways and our human thoughts. If we follow them, we will see God use our lives to influence others to follow Jesus.

Thoughts to Remember

Here are some closing thoughts to remember:

1. The teachings of evolution and humanism beginning at the turn of the 20th century affected godly moral values and exalted man's opinion above God's.

31

However, God's moral absolutes have never changed. They are contained in His Word.

2. The evolution teaching emphasizes that there is no God and no moral absolutes. Evolution and humanism claim that each person determines their own morals and what is reality for them. They teach that others who believe in moral boundaries are narrow-minded and are bigots. They resent Christians saying that those who choose to live in sin are wrong. They believe all beliefs are equal and all values are equal and that no one has the right to say that the Bible is the only truth.

3. The underlying agenda and motive of humanism and evolution teaching is to "cast off all restraint" in order to live by one's lusts. Aldous Huxley, an influential evolutionist, said, "The philosophy of meaninglessness was essentially an instrument of liberation. The liberation we desired was simultaneously liberation...from a certain system of morality. We objected to the morality because it interferred with our sexual freedom...."[7] This changing view of morality has worked its way into the church. Some Christians have been affected by it and maintain a liberal view regarding freedom from moral boundaries. As Christians, the Word of God tells us we have a responsibility for others who are a part of our lives, and what we do influences them in a right way or in a wrong way.

4. You can still dress stylish while establishing some restraints upon the way you wear your clothes.

5. When you live submitted to the Holy Spirit and to God's Word, you will do the right thing.

Endnotes

1. Fritz Ridenour, *So What's the Difference?* (Ventura, CA: Regal Books, Gospel Light, 1967, 1979, 2001), 174-175.

2. Janet Pearson, "Whose Values?" *Tulsa World*, October 30, 2005.

3. Aldous Huxley, *Ends and Means, First Edition* (Harper, 1937), 270.

4. Ibid., 272-273.

5. David King Dunaway, *Huxley in Hollywood* (Harper & Row).

6. Finis Jennings Dake, *Dake's Annotated Reference Bible* (Lawrenceville, GA: Dake Bible Sales, 1963, 1991), OT, 549.

7. Huxley, 272-273.

Chapter Three

Been There—Done That
(My Own Awakening)

YOU'VE probably heard this statement before: "Been there, done that, bought the picture." I can personally say that I've been there, done that, and I even have a picture of myself in the short dress and the skimpy shorts. It was the early 1970s. I can honestly tell you that I was *clueless* that guys have any difficulty with what girls wear. All I knew was that, like any other girl, I wanted to wear what was "in style." I believe there are many girls today as well who are as clueless as I was regarding how boys perceive them.

My own realization to the clothes issue came after I had had a spiritual awakening to Jesus Christ. Oh, I grew up going to church, and my father was my pastor. It wasn't like I didn't have a God consciousness; I had just never truly surrendered my life to Jesus Christ. I loved and respected my parents, and I wasn't a bad kid. I didn't do drugs, alcohol, or sex outside of marriage. I enjoyed having fun and basically lived my life the way I wanted.

I knew how to act according to whomever I was with in order to look good. (Note: I know a lot of youth and adults today in evangelical/charismatic churches who do this very same thing. Some of them are actually involved in drugs, alcohol, and sex but have learned how to live under a cover-up. One day the cover will come off.)

The Jesus Movement Changed My Life

Then in 1970, my life was seized by God. In fact, a lot of teenagers across America experienced drastic conversions in their lives. I later found out that this era became known as the "Jesus Movement." During this time, young people all over America were "moved," not only to surrender their lives to Jesus to be saved, but many were also supernaturally delivered from drugs, alcohol, sexual immorality, and rebellion. In addition, many of us responded to the call of God into ministry.

This movement came during the latter part of the "Hippie Movement," a revolt of the younger generation against "the establishment." It was fueled with riots and large groups of young people attempting to take over and rebel against whatever had been established in society, and also making every effort to remove boundaries, laws, structure, and order.

I remember the National Guard being called in to assist police in controlling riots and removing hippies from destroying and taking over people's private property. Hippies felt that all land should be free for anybody to do whatever they wanted to do with it. (Anytime people are under the influence of drugs and alcohol, destructive behavior follows. Drugs and alcohol remove self-restraint and sound reasoning. They influence people to do things that they would not do in their right mind.)

Disillusioned young people who had strict authority with no love at home, or who had parents who were divided regarding how to raise their children with boundaries, or who had parents who established no boundaries at all, were acting out their frustrations in open rebellion. Some were youth who had parents who had given them everything except love and time. Some were youth who were frustrated with the hypocrisy and lies they saw among adults and those in authority positions.

During this time of open rebellion—of drugs, alcohol, and "free love" (sexual freedom), of the removal of prayer and Bible reading from public schools, and "casting off" of moral restraints; God moved by His Holy Spirit. Hippies along with multitudes of other people got saved—I mean, really, radically, all-out-for-Jesus saved.

I was 16 years old the night I surrendered my life to Jesus Christ. I heard the voice of God for the first time speak three things to me in my heart and in my thoughts: "Read your Bible every day; pray each day; I've called you to minister to people." I remember feeling my life was no longer my own. At this point, nothing mattered to me except I knew I would obey God. All I wanted to do from then on was live for Jesus.

Day by day my life began to change. My desires and my thinking changed. And God started dealing with me about my clothes. If you think God doesn't care about the clothes you wear, think again. Once He sets up ownership in your life, He starts working on everything.

Listening to Your Conscience

When you develop a personal relationship with Jesus and He becomes more than a historical figure, you'll learn that He talks to you personally in your thoughts and in your conscience. It seemed that my conscience became supersensitive to things that hadn't bothered me before but now began to affect me. When you really surrender to Jesus and commit yourself to live for Him, your conscience is cleansed and becomes sensitive to God's voice in order to please Him (see Heb. 9:14).

Your conscience (*suneidesis* in the Greek) is the knowledge or principle within you that shows you what is right and wrong;

it is the power within you that decides the lawfulness of your actions and desires (or affections) and approves or condemns them; it is a moral sense within a person, also known as the eye or judge and guide of the inner man.[1] You can either listen to your conscience or ignore it. If you do ignore it, you will eventually experience trouble. Some have even lost their lives.

Remember the fiction story of Pinocchio? Pinocchio was a naive, curious little wooden boy puppet (made without strings) who wanted to experience a world beyond his own. One day he decided to run away. In doing so, he left his creator who loved him as a father and ran away from the security of boundaries and the love of someone who knew the cruelties beyond his house. Even though his conscience tried to persuade him not to go, he chose to ignore it, and his stubborn will and curiosity won.

Stubbornness and curiosity can get you into a lot of trouble. Pinocchio was lured, seduced, deceived, and hurt, until finally, in total discouragement, he listened to his conscience and made a decision to escape from his slavery and return to his creator. Even though he was swallowed by a whale when he decided to do what was right, in the end, he and his creator were united. He never ran away again.

The story of Pinocchio has a sweet ending of restoration, but this is not always the case in the real-life stories of many people.

Did you know that if a Christian ignores the voice of the Holy Spirit within his thoughts or conscience over and over again, his heart can become hardened? (see 1 Tim. 4:1-2; Heb. 3:7-15.) And *hardness of heart leads to deception even when a person is attending church regularly*. Whoa! That's something to think about. Hardness of heart and deception then lead to loss and destruction. This is why it's important that our hearts remain sensitive to God and to others.

The conscience of the Christian guides us to stay within moral and ethical boundaries. God's Word encourages us to do everything possible to maintain a good conscience. First Timothy 1:19 says, *"Holding faith, and a good conscience; which some having put away concerning faith have made shipwreck."*

The surrendered Christian who listens to his conscience will have a sense of restraint within, which includes knowing what styles of clothing are appropriate to wear and which styles are not.

I Became Aware of the Clothes I Wore

When God began to deal with me about changing the fashion trends I was wearing, it was as if someone was gently nudging me to evaluate the clothes I was wearing. Because my family was somewhat conservative, I didn't wear halter tops or the no-bra style or the miniskirts (barely covering the underwear), but I did wear skirts and dresses that were "short enough," low-slung hip-hugger bellbottom jeans, and the short shorts, better known as "hot pants."

During the early '70s the fashion trend for special occasions and parties was the infamous "hot pants" and matching jackets, accessorized with fishnet or textured hose and, of course, go-go boots. These items were what all the girls at school wore. While there was nothing wrong with the fishnet hose and go-go boots (except for the fact that they were extremely uncomfortable, even painful on the feet, to wear—it's amazing what we will do to look like everyone else), God did begin dealing with me about the short shorts and the short skirts and dresses.

I felt a need within me to tell my mom and even my boyfriend (who is now my husband) that God had told me to change the length of my dresses and shorts. Of course, my mom was glad, which was no surprise, but unexpectedly, my boyfriend (who had also been saved a few weeks after me) said he was relieved because it had been difficult for him. That was the first time that I realized how much guys struggle with what girls wear.

When a guy sees a girl dressed in a way that reveals or accentuates her body parts, immediately he must deal with imaginations and decide whether or not to continue to think about those imaginations or remove them by purposely rejecting them.

Attracting a Quality Man

Most girls don't realize that guys are *visual*. Unlike females, males are created with testosterones that, as they mature, can be easily triggered simply by looking at a female who is dressed in a way that accentuates parts of her body. *Guys have much more difficulty with what they see than girls do.* When a girl sees some guy without a shirt on, it may not create any arousal to her sexual desires. However, if a man sees a woman immodestly dressed, with her breasts or belly or a lot of leg showing, he can be sexually aroused immediately. It's part of the difference of our makeup as male and female.

When girls dress in whatever is fashionable, many of them have no comprehension of or consider what guys have to deal with in their minds. When a guy sees a girl who is wearing tight-fitting, revealing clothes, he wonders in his mind if she is saying, "Come and get me. I want you to have whatever you want and see." Whereas a girl may think she is simply dressing fashionably.

When a girl makes an effort to dress modestly and still stay within fashion, a guy is more likely to think, *She is secure in who she is and obviously isn't trying to find her identity in showing off her body and what she's got. She knows what she's got and she's saving it for the right one whom she'll marry one day.*

Over the years, I remember hearing about young guys who weren't saved or even thinking about God make comments like,

"That girl who is showing her stuff is who I'd like to play around with, but that girl [pointing out the one who was dressed more modestly] is the kind of girl I want to marry." Why is that? I'll tell you why. *The girl showing her body represents someone to use and throw away. The girl who is covering herself represents something valuable that the guy wants to someday possess and keep. Ask yourself, "Am I going to be a cheap throwaway, or do I want to be a valuable prize to be treasured?"*

A secure guy, not a "body hunter," is attracted to the strength of a girl who sets her standards and doesn't cave in to his or anyone else's peer pressure. She's not pressured by the put-down comments of other girls who talk that way, attempting to raise their own value. She's also not pressured by the manipulative persuasiveness of some slick-talking guy. She's discerning, and she possesses a strength within to stand up to criticism. She knows how to look good while staying within boundaries when she dresses. The quality guy then is not attracted to her for her outward decorations as much as he is to her inner strength, her love, her "realness," her sincerity, her genuine love for others, and her desire to please God.

Warning: *If you want a guy to want your body, you'll get a guy who wants only your body. He will get what he wants from you, and then he'll look for another body that he sees and wants.* If a guy marries a girl for her body, he'll continue to lust for any attractive body that he sees, even after he is married.

I've counseled women whose husbands married them out of lust; consequently, these women have to constantly deal with the insecurity of wondering if their husbands are cheating on them or not. They also struggle with the absence of closeness in their marriage relationship, except for sex. This produces a sense of no value except for her body. Over a period of time, this can cause resentment, bitterness, and a loss of any intimate love toward that husband. The marriage then becomes just an existence together.

When we focus our relationship with the opposite sex on our physical body and sensual clothes, it will be based on lust. Subsequently, whatever you obtain by lust, you'll pay for with heartache and pain, because lust is never satisfied. It always wants more and will look anywhere in order to get more.

Daily Surrender

As I grew in my relationship with Jesus, it seemed that my surrender and submission to Him was a regular necessity in my life. Still today, I realize that I have to daily surrender and submit myself to Him. In fact, His Word tells me that I have to "keep" myself so that the wicked one can't touch me (see 1 John 5:18). I am to keep that which I have committed to Him until He returns again. I am aware of the world around me that says, "It's okay to dress immodestly. It's fashionable and everyone else wears tight and revealing clothes. Besides that, you just can't find anything decent that is 'in style' anymore." Of course, these excuses are made by those *who don't really want to find clothes that cover up.*

I am also aware of the still small voice of God that lives within me, speaking to me His ways and His boundaries, I have to choose if I will follow His voice or the world's. And if I have to buy a size larger in order to be modest, then I will. Some girls and women insist on one size always. But if you need to wear a size 10 instead of a size 8 then just give up and do it. When it comes to pleasing God and not creating lust, who cares what number is on the tag?

Surrender is the only way any of us can keep growing spiritually in our walk with Jesus. Some people see surrender as a one-time event or a one-night fling of relationship and emotional ecstasy. Then the next day, they go on to live their lives the way they want to—with no sense of responsibility to change. Some see salvation only as a ticket to get to Heaven; but just as Jesus laid down His life for us, He also expects us to lay down our lives for Him (see Luke 9:23.)

I've come to recognize that getting saved is similar to getting married. (In fact, Ephesians chapter 5 parallels the relationship of Jesus Christ and the Church [Christians] with a husband-and-wife relationship.) When two people get married, they then must consider what the other person's needs and desires are. *When you become a Christian, you are married to Jesus, and as His Bride, you now consider what Jesus wants and needs from you. It's a lifetime commitment.*

I remember before I was married, I had met a young Christian married couple who agreed to date other people after they were married. Even as a young Christian, I knew that situation was "goofy." Needless to say, their relationship ended in divorce. They didn't want to let go of their desire for "freedom," even though their desire for freedom caused them hurt, pain, and loss. When Christians don't settle Jesus' lordship in their lives, their lust and flesh will lead and direct them until it ultimately destroys them. But when a person begins laying down his or her life for Jesus, the desires of the flesh will be denied, deprived of power, and submitted to God. In other words, you "starve it to death." Time with God in His Word and in prayer each day will allow the Holy Spirit to subdue the flesh.

At the same time, your *will* (which is a powerful part of you) will be convicted and pressed by God to submit to God's will. Jesus showed us in the garden of Gethsemane that through time in prayer, the will of a human can become submitted to God's will (see Matt. 26:36-42.)

Jesus' lordship within our lives is directly related to whether or not we allow His Word and His Holy Spirit to rule our lives. Lordship will be reflected through an attitude of humility and submission. The result will produce purity, truthfulness, and obedience to God. He will convict us and change us as we stay yielded to Him.

Yielding to Him means staying within the boundaries of His Word and His Holy Spirit's leading. Those who choose to live by the Word of God will turn away from the world's trends and way of thinking, which says that we should always be comfortable, happy, and fit in with everyone else. The cross is all about surrender—surrendering our wills to God's will. If we choose to take up our cross and follow Jesus, we will have to surrender and deny ourselves in some way. But when we live in surrender and submission to Him, we won't view the Word of God and His directions as laws and rules. Instead, we will see His Word as an instruction manual teaching us how to live and how to escape heartache and destruction (see 2 Pet. 1:3-4).

Thoughts to Remember

Here are some closing thoughts to remember:

1. Jesus' lordship within our lives is all about living in surrender. It is directly related to whether or not we allow His Word to rule our lives. Time in God's Word and prayer each day allows the Holy Spirit to subdue the flesh or deny its desires and power. Your will (which is a powerful part of you) will be convicted and pressed by God to submit to His will.

2. When Jesus is on the throne of your life, then the Holy Spirit will direct you in ways that produce pure thoughts and godly desires.

3. Hardness of heart can happen to a Christian who ignores his conscience over and over again. You must

hold onto your conscience. It is the knowledge or principle within you that shows you what is right and wrong; it is the power within you that decides the lawfulness of your actions and desires (or affections) and approves or condemns them; it is the moral sense within a person also known as the eye or judge and guide of the inner man. Ignoring your conscience can lead to trouble and can cost you your life.

4. Guys are *visual*. They have much more difficulty with what they see than girls do.

5. The girl showing her "stuff" represents someone to use and throw away. The girl covering her body represents something valuable that a guy wants to someday possess and hold forever. Ask yourself, "Am I going to be a cheap throwaway or a valuable prize to be treasured?"

6. A secure guy, not a "body hunter," is attracted to the strength of a girl who sets her standards and doesn't cave in to peer pressure.

7. When you focus your relationship with the opposite sex on your physical appearance, it will be based on *lust*. Subsequently, whatever you obtain by lust, you'll pay for with heartache and pain, because lust is never satisfied. Once it gets what it wants, it will desire more and will look anywere else to find what it does not have.

Endnote

1. Dake, NT, 236.

Chapter Four

The Emotional Rush of Lust

MOST of the time when the word "lust" comes to mind, people automatically think of men lusting for women. However, have you ever stopped to consider the fact that women can lust to be lusted for? You may have never thought of it that way, but guys know when a girl is naive or when she is purposely wearing clothes to seduce them. I've talked with both young men and older men…and they know.

A woman can experience an emotional rush of lust, knowing she has turned a man's head her direction to get a second look or even when he follows her with just his eyes. It can even become a game she plays on a regular basis because she craves attention. Women can be just as guilty of the sin of lust as the men who lust for them. Of course, they have the ability to play innocent, and this is where the sin of deception comes in.

I remember hosting a youth gathering of guys and girls at our house where one girl walked in with a tight, short top revealing half of her stomach and belly button, and hip-hugger pants that hung so loose it appeared they might fall off. They were unbuttoned in the front so that you could see her flowered bikini underwear. When my daughter spoke to her about it, she said, "Oh, I didn't have anything of my own to wear tonight, so I borrowed a pair of my sister's jeans and they're a little big on me."

Then when she was asked why she had them unbuttoned in front where her underwear was showing, the girl shook off the question by saying, "Oh, that's just my bikini swimsuit bottom I'm wearing underneath." My daughter replied, "You need to button up if you're going to stay here for the gathering." She did button up, but she kept hanging her hands on the sides of her pants so they would still look sexy. The true motive of her heart was to draw guys' attention to that part of her body for sexual arousal. She lusted to be lusted for.

When a girl or a woman lusts to be lusted for, she doesn't want anyone telling her what to wear or how to wear her clothing because she feels she should be free to do what she wants to do. Is this freedom—the ability to do whatever you want to do regardless of how it affects other people? Just to set the record straight—freedom in Jesus Christ is not freedom to do whatever you want to do. That is called lust and lawlessness.

Free From Lust

"Lawlessness" is not having any moral restraint; or having no restraint over your passions or desires. *Freedom* in Jesus Christ means you are free from the dominion and control of your passions. It is being free from the power of sin to manipulate you and free from going your own way. It is a freedom within your spirit that you no longer live by lust's control, but instead by the leading of the Holy Spirit.

When lust controls you, it will entangle you deeper and deeper until you feel you can't change or go another direction. Of course, that is a lie. That's exactly what satan wants you to think. The truth is, *Jesus Christ can deliver anyone who **wants** to be free from lust's dominion.*

Let's define "lust." *Lust* is to have strong desire or craving; a longing for; with the mind made up that if circumstances afforded opportunity, the person would commit an act of immorality. Lust is a state of heart and is as deadly as the act of immorality itself.[1] *"But I say unto you, That whosoever looketh on a woman to lust after her hath committed adultery with her already in his heart"* (Matt. 5:28).

Do you crave to be looked at? Do you enjoy the thrill of knowing that guys are being sexually aroused by how you look? Some girls are satisfied with just the thrill that they can turn a guy's head or his eyes, but this attitude can become lust. To be lustful is to provoke or excite those sensual passions in oneself and in others.[2] A girl can get "turned on" sexually knowing that she is turning on a guy sexually.

A person may say she is a Christian, yet if she uses no self-restraint toward creating thoughts of lust, impurity, and sexual desires outside of marriage, she is as dangerous as a poisonous snake. And anybody with a thimble full of common sense avoids poisonous snakes so that they don't get bitten and die. However, many who claim to be Christian see nothing wrong with lust and being sexually involved with other people outside of marriage.

Galatians 5:19 says, *"When you follow your own wrong inclinations your lives will produce these evil results: impure thoughts, eagerness for lustful pleasure"* (TLB) Colossians 3:5 says, *"Have nothing to do with sexual sin, impurity, lust and shameful desires..."* (TLB).

There are forces pulling you—in a right direction or in a wrong direction. Understand that when *you* are on the throne of your life, your inclinations will direct you selfishly toward fulfilling your passions, lust, and desires. On the other hand, when Jesus is on the throne of your life, the Holy Spirit will incline you toward pure thoughts, right motives, godly desires, and a fear of the Lord. You realize that God's eyes *"are in every place, beholding the evil and the good"* (Prov. 15:3). Nothing is hidden from Him, and you will reap whatever seeds you sow.

Living by Another Standard

Once when I was speaking to a group of young Christian teens about "The Surrendered Life and Living in Modesty," one of the girls raised her hand and asked if she could speak. I called her up to the platform and she shared her story. She began by saying, "You all know me. You know how wild I was when I first came to this church." She went on to say that shortly after coming to church, she surrendered to Jesus Christ and He began changing everything in her life. She said she realized immediately that her clothes had to change.

I thought it was interesting that no person told her that she needed to change her wardrobe; it was God who convicted her because she was now open to listen to Him and obey Him. I believe one of the signs of true conversion is when a person surrenders her life and she immediately wants to please God in everything. This new desire to please God seems to open a person up to God's voice, and there is a yearning to obey Him instantly without argument.

When she looked in her closet, she realized that all her clothes were tight, revealing, or short. She had shown a lot of skin. So she went through her closet and got rid of the clothes she had been wearing. Her mom then went shopping with her to buy some looser and longer shirts and shorts that summer. She also enrolled in our Christian school for the upcoming year.

During that summer, she usually went to the mall weekly, and she came to realize that no guys were noticing her. One time when she came home, she asked, "Mom, am I ugly?" Her mom answered, "No, you're beautiful. Why do you ask that?" She explained that previously, boys she didn't even know used to come up to her at the mall and ask for her name and phone number, but now, not one boy approached her. Her mom said, "Well, you're not wearing the clothes you once wore."

She said, "I realized then that the only guys I was attracting were the ones who wanted me only for my body." Then she said, "I also realized I liked all their attention and craved it as much as they craved looking at me. It was an adjustment. Everything Pastor Sharon is saying today is true. Girls and women wear the sexy fashion of clothes because we have had as much of a desire for guys to look at us as they have had looking at us." She realized her value didn't rest in her outward appearance. Her transformation as a Christian made her stand up against the crowd and challenge others to live by a different standard.

What Do You Want to Be Valued For?

Many Christian girls are still caught in or are struggling with the trap of thinking that their value is in their bodies. The oddity of this is that these same girls who dress in a revealing way, drawing attention to their breasts, bellies, legs, or bottoms, also desire to be treated with respect. They want people to value them for who they are as a person and not just as an object to look at. But while they want to be valued for their abilities and knowledge, others find it hard not to focus on their breasts, bellies, legs, or bottoms, especially when so much of these parts are forced in their faces. It becomes difficult for the person to get past looking at the tight and revealing clothes in order to listen to them speak.

Around our house, our sons have had lots of friends who come over and talk. I've had several discussions with many of these young Christian men who have told me that they often have to look up at the ceiling or sky or turn their heads to the side while talking to Christian girls or women who dress immodestly or seductively. Unfortunately, Christian guys of all ages have also shared with me that they have had difficulty even going to church and keeping their thoughts pure when Christian girls and women wear tight-fitting, low-cut, or see-through clothes to attract attention to their bodies. They feel they have to be on guard continually—even at church. But shouldn't church at least be a safe place for a guy's mind?

If a woman is secure in herself, she won't feel the need to keep creating opportunities to excite the sensual passion in guys. If she isn't secure, she will lust to be lusted for. If a young girl hasn't had a good father, guardian, or older brother to guide her and give her love and affirmation growing up as a child, she will seek to find love, affirmation, and value from a boy through the way she dresses. She will even go beyond moral boundaries for attention, acceptance, and love by a boy. As she grows up and then marries, she will still be trying to establish her value by how she looks.

One young Christian wife and mother who had gained a lot of weight during her pregnancies decided to lose weight simply because she wanted more attention. When she eventually lost weight, she bought new clothes to replace her other clothes. The new ones she bought, were tighter and formfitting. She began to draw attention from men and she liked it. She thought this made her feel valuable. In the beginning, it was just flattery. However, something changed within her. The thrill of attention and her desire to experience the world finally led her to leave her spouse and children in order to date other men and fulfill her lust.

The Devastation and Destruction of Lust

It has been said, "Lust will take you further than you want to go, cost you more than you want to pay, and keep you longer than you want to stay."

Lust can't be satisfied. It may appear to be appeased at times, but it is only a temporary satisfaction, and will soon rise up and say, "Give me more." James 1:15 says, "*When lust hath conceived* ["conceived" means to form an idea in the mind; to imagine], *it bringeth forth sin: and sin, when it is finished, bringeth forth death.*" In order to escape those consequences, lust must be "deprived of it's power" (see Col. 3:5 AMP).

Temptation starts with a thought. Then, if a person meditates on that thought, sooner or later the person is drawn away from self-control and steadfastness to entertain the thought. Lust begins when a person delights in the thought instead of rejecting it or turning away from it to another direction. When a person continues to hold on to lustful thinking, ultimately he or she will act out their lust. If not repented of, cut off, and changed in one's thinking, sin will ultimately bring destruction, loss, and sometimes death

This is why lust is not some small thing that a person can pass off as "no big deal." Lust's ambition is to take over your life. Lust convinces you that everyone does it, it's okay, and you will never suffer for it. If everyone does it and it's okay, then why would God say over and over to crucify lust, deny its way, deprive it of its power, give it no opportunity, and flee from it?

Here's a thought. If everyone told you that it's okay to jump off the Empire State Building because everyone is doing it, would you do it? Let's hope your answer is "No!"

Thoughts to Remember

Here are some closing thoughts to remember:

1. Women can get an emotional rush from men looking with desire toward them. Women can be just as guilty of the sin of lust as the men who lust after them. They lust to be lusted for.

2. Freedom in Christ doesn't mean you are free to do whatever you want to do. That's lawlessness. Lawlessness is not having any moral restraint, or having no restraint over your passions or desires. Freedom in Christ means you are free from the dominion and control of your passions and lust, free from the power of sin to manipulate you, and free from going your own way. Freedom in Christ will cause a person to desire to be led by His Holy Spirit. His Holy Spirit then will convict us of what is holy and what isn't holy.

3. Lust is to have a strong desire or craving; a longing for; with the mind made up that if circumstances afforded the opportunity, the person would commit an act of immorality. Lust is a state of heart and is as deadly as the act of immorality itself. In Matthew 5:28 Jesus said, "*That whosoever looketh on a woman to lust after her hath committed adultery with her already in his heart.*" Are you causing guys to commit adultery in their hearts? Are you committing adultery in your heart by lusting for them to lust you? Lust will take you further than you want to go, cost you more than you want to pay, and keep you longer than you want to stay.

4. A girl can be turned on sexually knowing that she is turning on a guy sexually.

5. When you are on the throne of your life, your inclinations will direct you selfishly toward fulfilling your passions, lust, and desires. When Jesus is on the throne of your life, the Holy Spirit will incline you toward pure thoughts, right motives, goals, desires, and a fear of the Lord.

Endnotes

1. Dake, Matthew 5:28, 4.

2. Noah Webster, *1828 American Dictionary of the English Language.*

Chapter Five

"In Your Face"—Legs, Breasts, Bellies, and Thongs

IT seems that most everywhere you go today you encounter "in your face" breasts, bellies, legs, or thongs. Stores sell push-up bras and low-cut blouses or dresses to emphasize the breasts; short tops and low-slung pants to expose the belly or waist area; miniskirts to reveal as much leg as possible; and tight pants and thongs so that those looking behind the girl or woman can easily tell that she isn't wearing normal panties. Instead she's wearing a string up the crack of her hips with a small amount of cloth showing above the top of her waistline outer clothing. Does this leave any question to a guy's imagination? Maybe only one and that would be, "Does she want me to follow her to a secluded place now to have sex, or later on after we get to know each other?"

Some may think I'm being ridiculous, but I have real-life stories to support what I am saying. I have counseled with girls and women who have been watched, followed, phoned, stalked, or raped, or they have friends who were.

Some girls and women think they can attract good-looking successful guys who want to rescue them in life, when in reality they are attracting men who have such severe problems with lust they would do whatever it takes to fulfill their desires. This is where most women don't stop and think. Although some girls and women have cried out against guys making sexual advances that they don't want, many of these same girls and women wear clothes that contradictorily cry out, "Come and get me."

Fashion designers say, "Show what you've got." But while you "show what you've got," there are others who are planning to take what you've got. For those who may not have thought about it, TV, DVDS, videos, movies, magazines, and even games are showing boys and men how to act out their desires and fantasies with girls and women who may be clueless. Wake up!

Because there is such an emphasis on showing breasts, we not only have push-up bras available in most department stores, but women also have access to cosmetic surgery to enlarge their breasts if desired. In fact, cosmetic surgery has become as commonplace as beauty shops. Girls and women can get larger breasts that stick out more so they will be noticed more. One Christian woman I know had surgery twice to enlarge her breasts and still lost her marriage, experienced depression, and said to me, "I feel like a freak because I have become so large." God still cares about her and loves her, but she's been through lots of heartache. I've also prayed with and have stood with other women who developed cancer from breast implants.

Then there's the "thong" thing. Thongs are on display in department stores for everyone to see and now for all ages of females. This may shock some of you, but stores now have thongs available for little girls (even preschool age) so that they can look sexy too. So let me ask, "Who wants little girls to be sexy?" Maybe sick-minded adults who are so full of their own lust they want to rob the pure innocence of childhood from a little one.

Twenty years ago thongs would have been found only in "sleazy" lingerie stores. Think about it! How far has our society gone? So what's the origin of the thong? Originally the thong was created for strippers and prostitutes. When thongs first appeared in department stores, only a few wives had the nerve to buy them for the bedroom only. However, as people have become more tolerant to seeing them displayed, more women, even single women, teen girls, and now little girls are wearing them for daily wear because *this is fashion*. What's wrong with this picture?

Why Wear Thongs?

Let me take a moment to say, thongs are not worn for comfort. Having a string running up the crack of your bottom is totally uncomfortable. Those who insist that they like them have had to wear them long enough to acquire a tolerance for them. It's similar to someone wanting to smoke a cigarette. I've been told that first smoking a cigarette tastes nasty, but because people want to be cool and accepted by others, they do it long enough to become accustomed to it..

A misconception that has been widely advertised is:"One size fits all." Here's a news flash: *One size does not fit all*. Short tops and low-slung pants and jeans that show bellies and belly buttons do not look the same on all bodies. Heavier girls with hang-over stomachs need to cover up because it is gross to look at. How about slim bodies? Exposing slim bellies is definitely sexier and much nicer to look at; however, when a girl shows her belly and her belly button, guys believe that she's communicating she will show more if conditions are right.

I've heard different reasons why girls wear thongs. One girl claimed,"Oh, I wear them because I don't want anyone to see my panty line."The thought that all she has on is a string and the rest is bare does more for a guy's imagination than a normal panty line. At least with a normal panty line, people know that she's wearing underwear and that she's not trying to let everyone know that she's wearing a thong. Besides, if you have a concern with a normal panty line showing under the pants, could it be that you need to check and see if the pants you are wearing are too tight? The tighter the fit, the more lines and bumps are revealed. Now, there's a thought.

People may not be able to see your panty line at the bottom of your hips. However, without trying to look, I have stood behind women and girls and noticed their thongs under snug-fitting pants. It was very obvious that the thong line went up the back of the bottom and revealed the lines of the top of the thong even under pants that went all the way to the waist. And girls who wear low-slung pants end up showing the top of the thong if their shirt is short or if they bend over slightly.

One lady told me that when a woman sat down in front of her at church, the top of her thong rose above the top of her pants in back and stayed there until another lady sitting behind her leaned forward to let her know it was showing and she should probably pull the back of her sweater down. Needless to say, she was embarrassed by the fact that a woman she did not know felt the need to say something to her. Correction does not feel good when it is given, but it can help us and deliver us if we don't resent someone having enough courage and love to warn us.

I've been told about one young Christian single man who had struggled with sexual fantasizing. He actually shared with a young woman how he watched the back of women at his church and could tell the ones who wore thongs and the ones who didn't. I've heard other guys who sit watch girls walk by and guess on the type of underwear they are wearing. You can't tell me that guys at church do not notice. There are godly guys who make every effort to look another direction, but there are some guys who struggle and are still pulled to look.

Causing Your Brother to Stumble

Since the fashion industry's goal right now is to promote wearing what looks sexy or attracts attention, Christian girls and women have to make a conscious decision who they will follow. If you are a follower of Jesus, you can't ignore His promptings directing you to avoid looking sexy or seductive. He will guide you not to cause your brother to stumble. You can complain and try to justify what you want to do, but if you live in surrender to Jesus, you will do whatever it takes to respect His presence—in your clothes, your behavior, your conversation, the places you go, the friends you hang out with, and your total lifestyle. You will realize that the fashion industry and the styles of the day are not the rulers of your life even though they may have changed the mind-set of our society.

Interestingly, what was totally unacceptable in public 50 years ago has now become the "norm" in our culture. Stop and think about it. Where will it be in another ten years? Twenty years? Will women be wearing anything?

I know of women even in ministry who have compromised in the way they dress, and it has caused other young women to think that it is okay to dress sexy for the public. Let me encourage you that sexy should be kept for the bedroom between a husband and a wife, not put on a platform to impress others, convincing yourself that you still have the stuff. Keep in mind that there are guys who are still struggling to conquer sexual temptation who come to church and in ministry settings who watch you like they watch every other woman on the street.

I've seen women who are middle-aged mothers at church who have a love for God, but who wear tight pants and tight tops to reveal their figure and the size of their breasts. One night at a church, I was standing behind a middle-aged woman whose pants were so tight in the back that you could see her thong line all the way up. She seemed totally unaware of it. I wondered why her husband had not noticed. If you are married, ask your husband to let you know if what you are wearing is too tight or revealing. Since most of us can't see our back, ask someone else to look and give their advice.

In October 2002, a youth pastor from another state was sharing with me that at a youth convention, one of the main speakers came to him with concern. He said, "I need youth counselors (guys and girls) to help me at the time I give an invitation. I've had difficulty with the way most of these Christian girls are dressed. I've never seen so many thongs showing when girls come and kneel, bending over to pray at the altar, as I have at this youth conference. It is forced in our faces."

Since the girls' blouses were short, every time they bent over even slightly, their pants would pull down and the top of the thong would rise so you could not help but see the girls were wearing thongs. The young man's statement was, "It was almost like a 'thong epidemic'!" and he asked other youth leaders, "What's happening? It's like modesty flew out the window."

I shared this story in an all-girls' meeting at the same time a separate meeting was being held for guys. Afterward, one young, 16-year-old guy, who had been raised in a Christian home with parents in ministry, heard the story I had shared and made the comment to a group of kids, "What right does she have to make girls feel uncomfortable wearing thongs? They should be free to wear whatever they want to wear."

Why was this young man so concerned about girls being able to wear thongs? Could it be that he liked girls wearing thongs because his own lust was gratified? If you stop and think, any godly guy trying to keep his thoughts and desires pure would thank me for addressing the matter. In fact, I've had other Christian guys (both young and old) ask me to speak to girls and women about the negative effects it causes for guys.

As a woman, a wife, a mother, a teacher of God's Word, and a pastor—modesty, purity, and morality *are* my business. If girls are ignorant as to what these words mean, then someone should explain these words to them.

At another time, I was at a college intramural football game when one of the Christian guys standing close by me with some other guys noticed some girls bending over beside him and said as he turned his head, "Oh, man." I then overheard him say to the other guys, "I wish the girls would not show off their thongs." This guy and the guys with him were leaders at that Christian university and were trying to keep their thoughts pure and help other guys they were responsible for to stay pure.

In light of everything we've discussed in this chapter thus far, the whole idea of wearing a thong so that no panty line or bumps can show, isn't substantiated. When a woman wears a thong, a man's imagination can go wild. The thong was created by fashion designers to arouse sexual thoughts. For sure, it was not created to cover anything or to help with modesty, nor was it made to be comfortable. Of course, a woman doesn't want to think about those things. But the fact is, when it comes to sexual arousal, a man can think through an entire sexual act with a girl or woman in a matter of seconds when he sees her wearing revealing clothes that show breasts, bellies, legs, or thongs.

Dress Yourself in a New Nature

Keep in mind that others watch you. Some watch to pattern their lives after you. Others watch with wrong motives toward you. Some watch with disappointment regarding what they are forced to look at. What you wear sends signals to people.

What do guys see when they look at you? Could what you are wearing be causing their imaginations to go wild? Jesus said in Matthew 5:27-30 (TLB):

*You shall not commit adultery...Anyone who even looks at a woman with **lust in his eye has already committed adultery with her in his heart**. So if your eye— even if it is your best eye!—causes you to lust, gouge it out and throw it away. Better for part of you to be destroyed than for all of you to be cast into hell. And if your hand—even your right hand—causes you to sin, cut it off and throw it away. Better that than find yourself in hell* (emphasis added).

These are very strong words. To clarify, Jesus is not saying here that He wants us to mutilate our bodies. People can mutilate their bodies and still have wrong thoughts and lusts. Rather, He wants us to cut off whatever situations are causing wrong thoughts and lust. His illustration shows us that we must become drastic in ridding ourselves of anything that creates lust and wrong thoughts in our lives. If you have a problem with lust toward others, cut off (get away from and avoid even the appearance of) any situation that would cause you to keep lusting for that person or lusting to be lusted for. If you have a problem with pornography, don't read pornographic magazines or watch pornography on TV, videos, movies, or the Internet. Get rid of anything that would tempt you toward it. If it is a person you lust for, get far away from that person. Jesus indicated that if you don't get rid of whatever causes you to lust and think sexual fantasies, it could take a person to hell.

I realize many Christians don't believe that sexual fantasizing is just as dangerous as the actual act. However, this is not what Jesus indicated. There has to be sincere repentance for a person to go to Heaven if he or she has had this pull toward sin. Besides, it has been said that whatever a person thinks about over a long period of time, they will ultimately act out.

In addition, we are commanded to never be the cause of another person sinning against God. Ladies, you could not only be causing guys to stumble by what you choose to wear, but you could be a factor in someone going to hell. Ask yourself if you are following the leading of the Holy Spirit regarding the clothes that you wear. Are you open to His correction if you need to be corrected?

Ephesians 4:17-24 (TLB) says:

Live no longer as the unsaved do, for they are blinded and confused. Their closed hearts are full of darkness; they are far away from the life of God because they have shut their minds against Him, and they cannot understand His ways. They don't care anymore about right and wrong and have given themselves over to impure ways. They stop at nothing, being driven by their evil minds and reckless lusts. But that isn't the way Christ taught you! If you have really heard His voice and learned from Him the truths concerning Himself, then throw off your old evil nature—the old you that was a partner in your evil ways—rotten through and through, full of lust and shame. Now your attitudes and thoughts must all be constantly changing for the better. Yes, you must be a new and different person, holy and good. Clothe yourself with this new nature.

When your motive for life is seeking to please God, lust will have no power over you. You'll think about what Jesus would want you to do. He definitely doesn't need you to wear a thong, show your breast cleavage, or wear tight clothes to reveal how big your breasts are or how cute your bottom is, in order to bring Jesus glory and honor. However, keeping yourself within the boundaries of modesty does honor God. It removes the possibility that someone might be seduced, and instead, they can hear what you have to say about Jesus.

Thoughts to Remember

Here are some closing thoughts to remember:

1. Although some girls and women have cried out against guys making unwanted sexual advances toward them, many of these same girls and women wear clothes that contractorily cry out, "Come and get me."

2. Evaluate what you wear. Although the world says, "Show what you've got," there are others who are planning to take what you've got.

3. The fashion industry's goal is to promote what looks sexy and attracts attention. Christian girls and women have to determine who they want to follow. Ask yourself, "Does Jesus need me, as His representative, to be seductive and sexy in how I relate to the world around me?"

4. Regarding sexual arousal, when a man sees a woman wearing revealing clothes that show breasts, bellies, or thongs, he can think through an entire sexual act in a matter of seconds.

5. Others watch you. Some watch to pattern their lives after you. Others watch with wrong motives toward you. Some watch with disappointment regarding what they see.

6. You could not only be causing guys to stumble by what you choose to wear, but you could be a factor in sending them to hell. Staying within the boundaries of modesty honors God and helps men in their attempt to follow Jesus.

Chapter Six

The Cause of Cold Sweats, Hot Flashes, and Rapid Heartbeats

The ANS

HAVE you ever experienced a sudden sense of danger and noticed your heart rate increase? This emotional and physical feeling is produced from the autonomic nervous system (ANS). Everyone has an autonomic nervous system.

"The autonomic nervous system (ANS) controls many organs and muscles within the body. In most situations, we are unaware of the workings of the ANS because it functions in an involuntary, reflexive manner."[1] Reactions such as rapid heart rate, an increase of pulse rate, a cold sweat, or a hot flash can occur when the ANS is stimulated. When someone experiences a sudden fear, ANS causes the heart rate to increase or blood pressure to rise without you pausing to think about it. You do not plan on your heart rate increasing; it just happens because the ANS is involuntary and acts in reflex to your environment. ANS is controlled by environment and not by a person's will.[2]

At times, ANS functions in a similar manner in both men and women, but there is one distinct difference. A girl's ANS is activated when she finds herself in a sudden situation of fear. It creates a rapid heartbeat, a cold sweat, or a hot flash momentarily. She doesn't have time to think about it. It happens suddenly as a result of circumstances.

In a male, the autonomic nervous system not only is activated in sudden fearful situations, but is also connected to his sexual system. This physical feeling or response throughout his body happens when he sees a girl or woman dressed in revealing clothes. He may break out in a cold sweat, or feel hot, or his heart may beat faster. Even though he may not have planned to be aroused, it still happens. I realize that some girls and women are oblivious to how they come across to guys. But then again, with the media daily bombarding the public nonstop with sex and skin, it's unlikely that many girls are as clueless as we might think them to be.

In an article in *Today's Christian Woman* magazine, Dannah Gresh states:

> Social science reveals a man's sexual response is initiated by his autonomic nervous system (ANS) which isn't controlled by the will but by the environment. If a man sees a woman walk by wearing revealing clothing, his ANS can be activated. The brain then sends chemicals rushing through his body. He may notice the change in his pulse and his body temperature. While many men override these responses in a godly manner, they can't control their initial intoxicating reaction to an immodestly dressed woman. God intends for a man to enjoy this intoxicating power but through only one woman—his wife.[3]

If a girl does not understand this part of a guy's makeup, she will have no regard for how she comes across to him. Having an awareness can help us be sensitive not to cause our brother to stumble or sin.

Capturing Our Thoughts

God created man from the beginning with this function inside of him to be attracted to a woman for the purpose of the marriage relationship. A guy can be walking along, thinking about his own business, round a corner, and suddenly be face-to-face with a girl who is wearing very little. That first reaction of his ANS will affect his heart rate and his blood pressure, causing reactions beyond his will. He then has to make a quick choice. He can immediately turn his head another direction to get control of his thoughts, or keep looking and long for what he sees. This is where his will to restrain himself comes into action or lies dormant. One choice delivers him from sin and the other choice causes him to sin.

It's important to know that a thought that comes to our mind does not become sin unless we embrace the thought or hold on to it. If a situation happens that suddenly brings a wrong thought to a person's mind, the person has the ability to allow it to remain or reject it immediately. Second Corinthians 10:5 says that we have the ability to cast down (reject) imaginations (thoughts) that try to come against the knowledge of God in our lives, and bring every thought captive to obey what Jesus Christ desires for us to think. The J. B. Phillips Translation says, *"Our battle is to bring down every deceptive fantasy..."* (2 Cor. 10:5). The New English Bible, New Testament Version says, *"We compel every human thought to surrender in obedience to Christ."*

We have the ability to capture our thoughts and make them think according to the Scripture. We can control our thoughts by speaking words such as "I resist the devil and his thoughts in Jesus' Name and I submit to God. I cast down every imagination or thought that exalts itself against God in my life and I bring my thoughts captive to obey God and His Word." Scripture and pray Scripture over our lives daily, we can overcome temptation and tests that come our way.

A person can choose to think pure thoughts just as Jesus thought pure thoughts. If he or she is suddenly confronted with a deceptive, seductive situation, this person can choose not to lust or think impurely and can turn away quickly from the situation in order to control their thoughts. At this point, they have not sinned or given into temptation. However, if the person holds on to a wrong thought, it becomes lust, and lust is sin—a sin that must be repented of.

If you, as a girl or woman, have noticed that some godly guys are avoiding you or if they have to look up or look to the side while listening to you speak, reevaluate your clothes and see if you could be dressing immodestly. Clue in to how godly guys act around you. If you are dressing in a way that is tempting them toward lust, they will be very cautious toward you.

Don't Copy the World

Today, in our society, fashion designers and media encourage girls and women to "show what you've got." Many Christian girls and women who attend churches seem to feel they need to "show what they've got" as well, desiring to look just like the beautiful, sexy, woman images they see in magazines, on TV, or in movies. The world's way of thinking has influenced Christians' thinking. Consequently, many Christians refuse to live with restraint. If someone points out that they need to dress more modestly, they sometimes get offended or claim that others are into "legalism."

Restraint is not legalism. Restraint is what Jesus referred to as "denying yourself" (see Luke 9:23). He said if anyone would come after Him and be a follower of Him, they would have to restrain and deny themselves in different areas of their life. On the other hand, lust has no restraints and no boundaries. Lust is a spirit that is controlling this world, whereas following Jesus means you are choosing to obey His words and His promptings instead of being conformed to this world's thinking and ways. Paul wrote in Galatians 5:16 that if we'll walk by the leading of the Holy Spirit, we won't fulfill the lust of the flesh.

Romans 12:2 says, "*Don't copy the behavior and customs of this world…*" (TLB). The world's way of thinking feeds the lust of the flesh. The world says, "Get rid of boundaries and restraints."

The fashion world and the media try to make you think that in order to be cool, in style, accepted, and even admired, you have to wear what they are selling. And because many Christian girls and women are not secure in themselves and in their identification with Jesus Christ, they accept the world's thinking and influence as the way it should be. Many young teenage girls don't give a thought about dressing to seduce guys, but rather dress to be in fashion and accepted.

"Showing off what you've got" may get you some attention at the moment, but relationships based on your physical body won't last, and there will be regrets and hurt feelings to deal with all along the way.

Leading and Learning With Love

When a young girl first starts to mature physically and develop some curves, there is an innocent excitement of becoming a young woman. The first time she is noticed for how she looks is a normal thrill. What a young girl and her parents have to protect is preventing her innocence from turning into lust. This can be guarded by what she views and listens to in the media and by making sure her friends have the same moral values that you have. Friends influence other young people regarding what they watch, read, or listen to in the media. This is why parents should know and talk to their teenagers about their friends' moral values. Helping a young girl understand and value herself, and set boundaries, should be motivated with love and not fear. Talk together about the effects and influence of music and the media. Talk about things without condemning her or her friends; give insight regarding why people do what they do and the consequences that result. She needs your love and affirmation more than ever—that you think she is beautiful, smart, and has the ability to make right decisions when she needs to. She needs your listening ear when she faces criticism and temptation, and your experience and counsel when she gives advice to help her friends. She also needs your trust. However, trust doesn't dismiss discernment. When you sense an uneasiness over something, communicate with her. Your listening, your words, and your responses can draw her closer to you or drive her further away.

Make sure you pray over your thoughts before you speak so that you are not operating in fear. When parents operate in fear, their words will sound like an attack instead of wise counsel. Love, however, will remove fear. A parent who takes time to pray and read the Word of God will experience an anointing of love upon the words that he or she speaks, even if they are words of correction and instruction. Initiate a conversation at times to explain the differences in how guys and girls think.

Make every effort to understand where she is coming from and what she is walking through. Let any words of advice be from an attitude of understanding and identifying with her situation so you can encourage her as you give her some helpful input. Instead of coming across as a forceful dictator, be a mentor who sincerely cares about her and a guide who has already been down the same road and knows the part of the path that has holes and ditches where a person could fall. I'm thankful for those mature guides in my life, even when I didn't realize they were guiding me.

Many Girls Don't Have Understanding of How They Are Coming Across

Often young girls do not understand how they come across to guys. When you are young, you've not had enough experience in life to understand and see the need to avoid vulnerability. When a guy sees a girl showing off her figure with tight-fitting clothes, short skirts, blouses that show some breast cleavage, and pants that reveal her navel, he is thinking she wants him not only to look but also to touch what he sees. He sees a sign that says, "Come and get me." Guys are turned on by sight as quick as you can flip on a light switch while girls are not programmed to be turned on as quickly, and they are not as stimulated by sight. Girls can look at guys without shirts and not be fazed. Sure, they might admire some muscle, but they aren't sexually stimulated by those muscles. They can become somewhat sexually stimulated, however, when they know they have stimulated a guy, and they experience even greater stimulation through touch.

A girl can think she's safe as long as *she* doesn't feel sexually stimulated. The problem with this thinking is that she is naively setting herself up for guys to "come onto her" and take what she didn't plan on giving away.

Remember the old saying, "Look but don't touch"? Nevertheless, guys are programmed to think beyond a look, and those guys who have already been exposed to lovemaking on TV or movies begin to fantasize in their minds. If they've been exposed to pornography, they struggle with undressing a girl in their minds while they are simply talking to the girl. The girl thinks she is being cute while he is thinking he wants to touch her where he shouldn't.

Reasoning Away What We Know Is Wrong

I remember reading a letter to "Dear Abby" in the newspaper about a couple in their 50s who had rented a duplex next door to a young couple. The young wife never wore underwear and her blouse always revealed the shape of her breasts as well as her nipples. The wife of the owner resented this woman's appearance each time the young woman talked to the older woman's husband because she knew that this woman wanted to sexually arouse not only her husband but any man she was around.

The writer of "Dear Abby" suggested that the couple who owned the duplex sit down with the young couple and inform them of this difficult situation, asking the young woman to dress differently. If she refused, she and her husband would need to find another place that would suit them better. I've likewise encountered Christian girls and women who obviously weren't wearing bras under their clothes, consequently revealing the form of their breasts and nipples. Anyone could tell by a glance that they were not wearing underwear. If it is difficult for the reader to understand, I'll make it plain. If a guy can easily determine that a girl or woman is not wearing any underwear, it triggers lust and fantasy in his mind if he doesn't look away or immediately remove his thoughts from it.

I've talked with Christian men of all ages—teens and adults—who have desired to walk holy, but who have had difficulty when Christian girls and women do not seem to be sensitive in the area of dressing modestly. At other times, a guy can reason away the importance of staying pure in his thought life by telling himself that every guy has wrong thoughts. Does that sound like a cop-out?

In the book, *Every Man's Battle*, by Stephen Arterburn and Fred Stoker, the authors point out that Christians who struggle with sexual impurity do so because they have diluted God's standard of purity with their own reasoning. Have you reasoned away sexual purity as no longer relevant today? Some Christians say, "Oh, well, we all sin in thought, word, or deed every day." They claim that people just can't keep from sinning. What they are saying is, "Go ahead and sin because you're going to sin in some way every day anyway." If it is okay to think wrong thoughts and okay to sin and not restrain yourself, then why did Jesus and the writers of the New Testament say we should cut off, deny, or kill wrong thoughts and not allow them? (See Matthew 5:28-30; Ephesians 5:3,5-8,11; Colossians 3:5; Romans 13:13-14; 6:11-16; 1 Thessalonians 4:3-8; James 4:4-8; 1 Peter 2:11.)

A girl likewise can reason away the importance of dressing modestly by telling herself that it's fashionable and every other girl and woman wears the same immodest clothes. In addition, "you just can't find modest clothes in stores anymore." Let me ask then, why are some Christian girls and women able to find fashionable clothes that are modest? Why do people still admire them even though they dress modestly? Why did Jesus and other New Testament writers write about purity, modesty, and living holy lives?

Many Christian girls and women feel they should be free to dress however they desire without having to consider some man's thoughts toward them. They think that if guys have a problem, it's *their* problem to deal with, and they shouldn't make girls feel that they can't dress immodestly.

"Am I My Brother's Keeper?"

Why should we be responsible for anybody else? Why can't we just live our lives and let others live their lives? Why should girls and women feel any responsibility for guys who struggle?

Let's consider the story of Cain and Abel who were the first two children of Adam and Eve. When Adam and Eve sinned and were removed from the Garden of Eden, the only way they could approach God's presence was by bringing an animal sacrifice. God gave them this direction so that the blood of their sacrifice would cover their sin.

Abel brought an animal sacrifice as he had been told, but Cain decided to bring his own works of what he had harvested. He did things his own way instead of God's way. Hence, God could not accept his sacrifice. Then, instead of repenting and doing as God had directed, Cain took offense and became angry, resentful, and jealous of his brother who had done the right thing and obeyed God's directions.

God tried to warn Cain that He could see that the bitterness within him was going to cause him to sin, but he wouldn't listen to His warning. Eventually, Cain murdered his brother Abel. Afterward, God came to Cain, and even though He knew what had happened, He gave Cain an opportunity to admit his sin by asking him, "*Where is Abel thy brother?*" (Gen. 4:9a). Cain's response was, "*I know not* [or we might say, "I don't know"]. *Am I my brother's keeper?*" (v. 9b).

Of course, we know that his response was, first, a lie because he knew where Abel was. Secondly, he did not take responsibility for his brother. But nevertheless, *God held Cain responsible, because he **was** responsible for his brother.* God said, "*The voice of thy brother's blood crieth unto Me from the ground*" (v. 10b). Subsequently, a curse came upon Cain because he would not repent.

Today many people like Cain do not want to feel responsible *for* anyone else or *to* anyone else. There's a desire for so-called "freedom" to do whatever a person wants to do, whether it affects others negatively or not. This attitude promotes the thought that if others are hurt, it's their problem and not our own responsibility. If we ignore our conscience that talks to us and tells us when we've done right or wrong, we can become hardened to any sense of responsibility toward others.

However, God still holds each of us as Christians responsible for others and how we come across to them. "Responsibility" is the state of being responsible or answerable for one's actions and decisions; being accountable when called upon to report or account for one's actions or behavior; liable (obliged or *bound by one's conscience*, by law, or by moral duty); to be called upon to answer for one's actions or decisions or thinking.[4]

Since we are still in the process of growing in our spiritual understanding and walking with God, sometimes we as Christians fail. However, responsible Christians are willing to see their failure, admit it, and correct it. Once they gain the appropriate knowledge and are made aware of their responsibility, they make an effort to do what is expected.

God's Grace Is No Excuse for Lasciviousness

The grace of God is a wonderful gift and one that we must not abuse. But the Scriptures say that ungodly people will try to turn *"the grace of our God into lasciviousness..."* (Jude 4). "Lasciviousness" in the Greek is *aselgia*, and it means "lustfulness; unchastity (being indecent in behavior, dress, and speech that encourages someone else to let go of their virginity or marital fidelity); *promoting or partaking of that which tends to produce lewd emotions, anything tending to foster sex sin and lust."*[5] Lasciviousness lets go of moral restraint. Some let go of moral restraint and say that it's OK God's grace covers it. Does the grace of God cover someone purposefully living lasciviously.

Is the way you're dressing *lascivious*? Do your outfits create sexual desires in guys when they see you? Does the way you wear your clothes cause a guy to imagine performing sexual acts with you? Ephesians 5:3 says, *"But among you there must not be even a hint of sexual immorality, or of any kind of impurity...*" (NIV). A *hint* is the smallest amount. Are you hinting anything by the way you dress?

Galatians 5:19-21 declares that if we are lascivious, we will not inherit the Kingdom of God. Christians who know that something is wrong but continue doing it with an attitude, "It doesn't matter, I'll still be saved," are self-deceived. God holds us responsible for the knowledge and awareness that we receive.

A friend shared with me that years ago she used to wear everything in fashion. She considered herself a "free spirit" and wore whatever she wanted to wear. When she got married, her husband at that time, who was led by lust, also wanted her to dress in a revealing way. She and her husband then got saved but didn't think anything about the way she dressed until one day when she was spending time with her unsaved sister.

The two women were running errands when she began to talk to a man about Jesus Christ and share her testimony with him. After driving away, the unsaved sister rebuked her and said, "How dare you talk to that man about Jesus, wearing a see-through fishnet blouse with some small lettering across your bustline, wearing no bra (revealing your breasts) and your tight short shorts that show some of your underwear!" Her unsaved sister had taken offense. Even in her limited knowledge of Jesus Christ, she knew Jesus was holy and that anyone claiming to be a Christian and wearing clothes that made a man look at her body while she was talking was wrong.

She said that the thought of her unsaved sister having more spiritual savvy than she did hit her like "a ton of bricks." She went home and told her husband she was getting rid of all her immodest clothes and would be buying other clothes that covered her. At first, he wasn't happy with her decision because he himself had a lust problem and liked her showing her body. Later he realized he was wrong. Over the years, they have allowed God to work in their lives, and though they've been tested, they've chosen to bring their lives into submission to God's Word and His standards. Today, they help counsel couples and have been used to bring freedom to those bound by lust.

If what we wear or how we come across to the opposite sex is causing them thoughts of lust, then we need to change. The Bible says if we realize something we are doing is wrong and yet we keep doing it, it is sin (see James 4:17). Sin is going our own way instead of God's way. When we repent of sin, however, we not only acknowledge to God that we have done wrong, but we also change our course of direction. We choose to do what is right and what will please Him.

Thoughts to Remember

Here are some closing thoughts to remember:

1. The autonomic nervous system (ANS) is involuntary and is controlled by environment and not by a person's will.

2. The ANS in males is connected to their sexual system. An immodestly dressed woman can activate a man's ANS.

3. Our eyes and ears are connected to our thoughts. Our actions or behavior are a result of our thoughts. "*Our battle is to bring down every deceptive fantasy...*" (2 Cor. 10:5 J. B. Phillips). The New English Bible, New Testament, says, "*We compel every human thought to surrender in obedience to Christ.*" We have the ability to choose or reject thoughts that come to our minds. Just because a thought comes to your mind does not mean you have to accept it. You can reject it,

cast it down, and replace that thought by speaking a Scripture, preventing yourself from sinning in your thoughts. A wrong thought becomes sin only if you embrace it and entertain it. If you reject it, you have rejected sinning.

4. Guys are turned on by sight while girls are turned on by knowing that a guy is looking lustfully at her and by a guy's touch. Some girls think that as long as they are not sexually aroused, they are safe.

5. In the book, *Every Man's Battle*, the authors Stephen Arterburn and Fred Stoker point out that Christians who struggle with sexual impurity do so because they have diluted God's standard of purity with their own reasoning. Some Christians say, "Oh, well, everyone sins in thought, word, or deed every day, so go ahead and sin because you are going to sin in some way daily anyway." If this is God's view, then why did Jesus and the writers of the New Testament say we should cut off, deny, or kill wrong thougts and not allow them? (See Matthew 5:28-30; Ephesians 5:3,5-8,11; Colossians 3:5; Romans 6:11-16, 13:13-14; 1 Thessalonians 4:3-8; James 4:4-8; 1 Peter 2:11.)

6. God calls every Christian to be responsible. Responsibility is being liable, obliged, or bound by one's conscience to answer for one's actions, decisions, thinking, and behavior. It is to be accountable. Do you feel responsible for others in how you live your life?

7. *Lasciviousness* in its original meaning in Jude verse 4 is promoting or partaking of *that which tends to produce lewd emotions or foster sex sin and lust;* unchastity (being indecent in behavior, dress, and speech that encourages someone else to let go of

their virginity or marital fidelity). Jude tells us that we're not to turn the grace of God into lasciviousness.

8. Ephesians 5:3 (NIV) says we're not to allow even a hint of sexual immorality or any kind of impurity. Are you hinting anything by the way you dress?

Endnotes

1. http://cc.msnscache.com/cache.aspx?q=20606 42955022&lang=en-US&FORM=CVRE. Accessed 7/22/05.

2. "Birds, Bees...and Sharks?" *New Man Magazine*, November/December 2003, 44-45.

3. Dannah Gresh, "A Decent Proposal," *Today's Christian Woman*, May/June 2003.

4. Noah Webster, *1828 American Dictionary of the English Language*. (This definition is drawn from Webster's definitions of "responsible," "liable," "accountable," and "obligated.")

5. Dake, NT, 207.

Chapter Seven

Boundaries Can Save Your Life

BOUNDARIES are limits.[1] They define an area that is forbidden to enter, or an area from which you should not leave. Think about a farmer who builds a fence around his property so that people cannot trespass on his property and take or destroy what doesn't belong to them. Similarly, your body is God's property and you are the manager over it; hence, it is your responsibility to ensure that no one trespasses, taking or destroying what doesn't belong to them. A person who neglects to establish boundaries in her life is setting herself up to be used, abused, and taken advantage of. *If you don't set the necessary boundaries, your body will become the property of someone who has no right of ownership.*

A Young Girl's Story

Without boundaries, a girl or woman today can not only be hurt but also destroyed. I remember listening to a woman share her own personal story. As a young girl of 12, she had already developed a figure that made her look like she was 15 or 16 years old. Of course, boys noticed her, and she liked the attention, but was sexually naive. When she was 14 or 15 years old, she started to give in to peer pressure. She had an older brother who had friends, and as they experimented with alcohol, she drank some too.

One night, three guys took her with them in a truck and drove to the woods outside of town. They took turns molesting her. She was brutally beaten until she could hardly move. At one point, she acted as if she was unconscious while they walked off to drink some more. She then cried quietly to God for His help. Although she didn't have a driver's license and really didn't know how to drive, she crawled into the driver's seat, naked, bleeding, hurting, and full of shame—and drove away.

Her parents weren't Christians, so she didn't receive the godly counsel she needed. And at the time this incident occurred, people just didn't talk about those kinds of shameful things. Meanwhile, her parents had become involved in the psychic realm. Searching for acceptance and identity, she also became involved in demonic activities. Amazingly, she seemed to exhibit power in this realm, so her parents and her psychic mentor planned to send her to a psychic school in Switzerland. (Note: When someone experiences sexual uncleanness outside of marriage, he or she can especially become prey to the demonic realm without realizing it.) However, at the last moment, she changed her mind. Instead, she went to live with her sister and her husband who had become Christians and had been praying for her and their family to be saved and delivered from demonic influences. She received Jesus Christ into her heart and renounced her past involvement in the satanic realm. Later, other family members also came to know Jesus as their Lord and Savior.

After she was saved, she realized that she needed to set boundaries in her life, because without them she was vulnerable to trouble. Years later, she also became aware that she had to instill boundaries in her children as well so that they could avoid the deceptions she had experienced. Over the past few years, God has used her to teach other girls and women how to set boundaries in their lives to avoid heartache, pain, and destruction.

Boundaries Are Good and Godly

There are many good boundaries in the earth that have been created by God. He created a boundary between the ocean and dry land. He created trees to grow to a certain designated height. He placed the sun at a specific distance from the earth so that the earth and its occupants would not burn.

We as human beings have also established many boundaries. For example, governmental agencies set limits or consequences to protect its citizens so that someone won't feel at liberty to destroy another person or his property.

On a personal level, I have placed boundaries over my own life, I have chosen to restrain myself in certain matters, and I have also chosen to restrain others from taking advantage of me. But to do this, I first had to think about how I dress, how I behave, and how others might view me. This isn't bondage; rather, it is protecting that which is valuable to me—my life.

Pure and Holy Perimeters

God's boundaries are set within the perimeters of that which is pure and holy, because God is pure and holy. He says, "*But be holy now in everything you do, just as the Lord is holy, who invited you to be His child. He Himself has said, 'You must be holy, for I am holy'*" (1 Pet. 1:15-16 TLB).

Holy means "to be set apart from secular or worldly use to be used for God's purposes; consecrated (or devoted and dedicated) to God; making a separation within yourself not to live in sin and immorality; purity of life and morals."[2]

Second Timothy 1:9 says that when we receive salvation, God calls us with a holy calling to live according to His purpose. He takes ownership of our lives; He becomes our Master and Lord; and we take the position of serving Him. His command to "live holy" requires us to submit to His authority, His rule, and His power in our lives. He wants us to pursue Him and His will more than our own fleshly desires.

Some confuse *righteousness* and *holiness*. Righteousness (or right standing with God) has been provided as a gift to us by Jesus' death and resurrection. We receive His gift of righteousness through faith in His cleansing blood. When we believe in Jesus and receive Him and His cleansing blood in our hearts, we are made right with God. That's righteousness. We didn't earn our salvation by our goodness. We received our salvation by faith in Jesus. *It's important to realize, however, that **God didn't save us by grace so that we could sin in style***.

There is a distinct difference and separation between people who really want Jesus and love Jesus from those who just want to hang around and see what they can get for free. Many Christians don't want to submit to a belief system that requires them to do anything but receive. They want benefits without commitment.

However, holiness is what God calls us to walk out in our lives here on earth. At the time we are saved, He separates us in our hearts to live for Him. He puts a desire within us to please Him. That's His holy calling. Hebrews 12:14 tells us we are to "***pursue** peace with all people, and holiness, without which no one will see the Lord*" (NKJV, emphasis added). Pursue means "to chase after; to follow closely." (The Greek word is *dioko*.)[3] It means "to chase; to imitate; to follow as an example; to seek; to go after in the same direction."[4]

In this Scripture, in order to chase after or closely follow Jesus' example of relating to others, we need to (1) walk in peace, and (2) walk in holiness. Holiness involves attitudes of our heart as well as our behaviour. A part of holiness is living at peace in your heart in how you relate to others. To be at peace with others means we cannot allow bitterness, unforgiveness, resentment, unresolved anger, strife, animosity, or hatred toward others. These are sins of the heart that must be removed from our lives in order to go to Heaven. Let me encourage you that God will help you if He sees you making the effort to overcome any of these heart issues. God looks upon your heart and knows when you are pursuing holiness and pressing hard to obey Him.

The other aspect of holiness has to do with our attitude and behavior regarding morality and purity. The Word of God shows us His will for living a holy, consecrated life with regard to controlling and denying sexual desires outside of marriage. God created us with sexual desires that He intends for us to keep within the boundaries of marriage. These boundaries are holy. That is why, when two people are married, it is called "holy matrimony." God places His hand upon the hands of the husband and wife and establishes a covenant relationship with them.

This holy covenant is a boundary of protection for sexual intimacy between a husband and a wife. It protects them from the emotional hurt, shame, and heartache of having sex outside of marriage and abandoning a partner for someone else. It protects them from sexual disease caused by having sex with several partners.

First Thessalonians 4:3-4,7-8 says:

*For God wants you to be holy and pure, and to keep clear of all sexual sin so that each of you will marry in holiness and honor—not in lustful passion as the heathen do, in their ignorance of God and His ways....**For God has not called us to be dirty-minded and full of lust, but to be holy and clean.*** [Wearing clothes that are revealing, too tight, or sexually arousing cause lust.] *If*

*anyone refuses to live by these rules **be is not disobey-
ing the rules of men but of God who gives His Holy
Spirit to you*** (TLB, emphasis added).

Paul says that when you choose not to live holy or in moral
cleanness, you are rebelling against God, which is a serious matter. First Thessalonians 5:22 tells us to remove ourselves even
from situations that might not be evil but might be perceived by
others to be morally questionable. Pursuing holiness means
avoiding even the appearance of evil.

Jesus said, *"Blessed are the pure in heart: for they shall see
God"* (Matt. 5:8). This word *pure* means "clean." (The Greek word
is katharos.)[5] As a girl pursues purity, she sets herself within
moral boundaries. She understands what it means to to restrain
herself and not allow herself to do that which is immoral. This
includes "lewdness (showing or intending to excite lust or sexual desire in another person; intemperance (indulgence in drinking alcohol), gaming (or gambling—betting on something or
playing a game for money); profaneness (not only cursing and
using God's name in vain, but also doing what is obscene); fraud
(taking advantage over another by lies and deception); and injus-
tice (violating another person's rights)."[6]

Pure means unmixed, or in other words, not being part of a
mixture of both the world and of God. When a Christian pursues
walking in purity, she is aware that she needs to keep her
thought life from being influenced by things which are impure,
unclean, and immoral.

Your thoughts are directly related to what you see and what
you hear. Your eyes and your ears are the doors into your mind
and heart. If you don't guard these doors, anything and everything will come right in. And if allowed to stay long enough, these
things will eventually make themselves at home and become
part of your household. Your thinking will turn into your behavior, which includes the clothes you wear. What you wear is a

result of those influences upon your thoughts, including what you see others wear, how they wear what they wear, and what they do.

A Friend of the World or a Friend of God

The world system of impurity, immorality, and lawlessness, which exists all around us, is constantly battling for your attention and wants to take over your life. So, in order to turn from the world's destructive ways and follow God's holy calling on your life, you must make a firm stand and resist the world's pull and influence. You can't be a friend with the world system and a friend with God at the same time.

We can *believe* that we are a friend of God and we can say that we are His friend, but does our life reflect that we are a friend of God? James 4:4 let's us see that those who want what the world has to offer but they also want God's blessing are actually going against God, "*You [are like] unfaithful wives [having illicit love affairs with the world] and breaking your marriage vow to God! Do you not know that being the world's friend is being God's enemy? So whoever chooses to be a friend of the world takes his stand as an enemy of God*" (AMP). In this passage, the writer, James, describes the feelings and emotions that God possesses toward a believer who transfers his devotion and passion from Him to the world. If a believer chooses to make her relationship with the world a greater priority than her relationship with God, she is making a choice that will put her in direct opposition to God. God takes this decision so personally that He views it as an act of war! To God, this is the ultimate violation![7] And God calls you an enemy.

"The word 'enemy' (*echthros* in the Greek) means enemies in a war or enemies in a military conflict. It is the picture of two nations who are in opposition to one another and have therefore engaged in a military conflict. They are warring nations. They feel hostility, antagonism, and even animosity for each other."

In Matthew 6:24 Jesus said, "*No man can serve two masters: for either he* [she] *will hate the one, and love the other; or else he* [she] *will hold to the one, and despise the other. Ye cannot serve God and mammon.*" "Mammon" was an expression used by the Jewish community of the New Testament times to express the idea of *worldliness*. So when Jesus said it was impossible to serve God and mammon, He was actually saying that it is impossible to serve both God and worldliness. [8]

You have to choose which one you want to live for and which you will allow to consume your thinking. The world wants you to become saturated with its thinking, views, fashion, and direction. *But God doesn't want to be just an "add-on" in your life. He wants to be your life's focus—number one*. He, likewise, wants total rule and influence over your choices, decisions, time, friends, activities...and even clothes. He wants control of your thinking, your views, your desires, and your directions. *He wants to be the sole influence in your life*. You are His. You belong to Him and He wants others to know it.

To close this chapter, I suggest that belonging to God can be compared to "going steady" with a guy. When a girl "goes steady," she dates no other one but the man she claims to love. Only he is always on her mind and she doesn't flirt with anyone else. Everyone else knows that she belongs to him. Likewise, when you belong to God, you're His girl. You don't flirt with the world and what it offers. You have only Him on your mind, and everyone else knows that you belong to Him.

Thoughts to Remember

Here are some closing thoughts to remember:

1. Boundaries are limits. They define an area that is forbidden to enter, or an area from which you should not leave. If you don't set any boundaries in your life, your body will become the property of whoever decides to take it.. A person with no boundaries in her life will be used, abused, and taken advantage of. Your body is God's property, and you are the manager over it

2. Boundaries are not bad. They're good and godly. God has created many boundaries.

3. God's boundaries are set within the perimeters of pure and holy.

4. From God's point of view, *seductive* and *holy* cannot be used in the same sentence. *Holy* means set apart from secular or worldly use, to be used for God's purposes; consecrated (or devoted and dedicated) to God; separating yourself in your heart not to live in sin and immorality but in purity of life and morals.

5. God didn't save you by grace so you can sin in style. Being made righteous is a gift we receive when we are saved. Holiness is a calling that God places upon our lives to pursue. *Pursue* means to chase after, seek, and follow closely; to imitate the example Jesus gave us.

6. God created you with sexual desires that He intends for you to keep within the boundaries of the marriage relationship.

7. Jesus said, "*Blessed are the pure in heart: for they shall see God*" (Matt. 5:8). *Pure* means unmixed—not being part of a mixture of the world and God. When

a person pursues purity, she understands she has to restrain herself from what is immoral.

8. James 4:4 says, "*Whoever chooses to be a friend of the world takes his stand as an enemy of God*" (AMP). Here, James is speaking about the worldly way of thinking and living. Jesus said in Matthew 6:24, "*No man can serve two masters: for either he will hate the one, and love the other; or else he will hold to the one, and despise the other. Ye cannot serve God and mammon.*" "Mammon" was an expression used by the Jewish community of the New Testament times to express the idea of *worldliness*. Jesus says that we cannot serve both God and worldliness. He wants total rule and influence in our lives.

Endnotes

1. *Webster's New World College Dictionary*, 165.

2. Noah Webster, *1828 American Dictionary of the English Language*.

3. Dake, NT, 255.

4. Noah Webster, *1828 American Dictionary of the English Language*.

5. Dake, NT, 4.

6. Noah Webster, *1828 American Dictionary of the English Language*.

7. Rick Renner, *Sparkling Gems From the Greek*, "Is It Possible for a Christian to Become the Enemy of God?" 436-437.

8. Ibid., 435-437.

Chapter Eight

Guarding Your Stuff

WHATEVER we determine to be valuable, we guard and protect and treat with care. Precious jewels, for example, are handled delicately and stored in a safe and protected place. Possessions that are rare, costly, or unique are hidden or covered so that no one can easily steal them.

Guarding Your Jewels

Let's imagine that you have been given a diamond ring, necklace, and earrings that are worth $500,000. Common sense tells you that you probably won't wear them out in everyday public life, such as to the store, a ball game, school, work, the gas station, or some other place you normally go. Most likely, you will not loan them to anyone, not even your closest friends.

Friends can be well-meaning, but sometimes they can be clueless and naive when it comes to understanding how valuable your jewels are and the seriousness of the need to guard them. There are others who may be friendly but they have a wrong motive in getting to know you. These people will try to convince you that they care about you and you can trust them, but they are deceptive and plan to take your valuables, sell them, and then keep the money for themselves. Then there are other people who don't even try to hide the fact that they want to take something from you. They're just waiting for the right time to find a way to get you alone, possibly molest you, knock you out, or kill you, then take your jewels.

Thieves can be male or female, young or old, good-looking or homely, sincere or tough. If you are not aware and watchful, to diligently guard and protect your jewels, it's likely you'll be robbed.

Your Body Is a Valuable Jewel

Think about it. Your physical body is a valuable jewel. Covering or protecting certain parts of your body will help ensure that those who are looking for an easy steal keep their distance. Smart thieves study people with valuables. They can determine a person of negligence or a person who is naive or who has a need for attention. They notice pride in anyone who likes to show their valuables to the public, and they watch for any indication of vulnerability from the owner who possesses the valuables. They plot and plan to steal what they want. Sometimes they will even go so far as to get to know the owner on a friendly basis in order to lessen the likelihood of being suspected as a thief. They may appear to really care about the person who owns the valuables, but actually they want to take all they can get and then move on to other easy prey.

A smooth-working guy will patiently watch a girl who flaunts her valuables (her body). He might attend functions that she attends in order to be introduced. After getting to know her, he pretends that he really cares for her, but the lust in his heart is what drives him. She thinks he wants a quality relationship with her that will last. But the only thing he is interested in is getting what he wants. Once he deceives her into giving him her valuables (giving him what he wants sexually), then he grows tired of her and moves on to another girl.

There Are Consequences for Showing Your Treasures

In Second Kings chapters 18–20, there is a story about a king named Hezekiah who ruled over Judah (Israel today, God's chosen people, the Jews), and as a king, he accomplished a lot of good things to improve the kingdom. He removed the worship of other gods, and he encouraged the people to follow after the Lord. Subsequently, God blessed him. Unfortunately, Hezekiah became proud of his victories and prosperity, which opened the door to sickness near death.

The prophet Isaiah, who had prayed with him previously and saw God's hand deliver the Israelites from their enemies, came to Hezekiah and told him to set his house in order because he was going to die.

When Hezekiah heard this, in humility and brokenness he cried out to the Lord for mercy to live. Isaiah the prophet, who was leaving as Hezekiah was praying, turned back and said, "God has heard your cry and He is healing you. You will have 15 years added to your life." Hezekiah was healed.

In the meantime, kings of neighboring countries had heard only of Hezekiah's illness and were anxious to take advantage of Hezekiah's *vulnerability*. The king of Babylon (which today is Iraq) was one of those who heard about Hezekiah's illness and sent his son and some men to determine his condition.

Hezekiah, thinking that the king of Babylon really cared and was concerned for his well-being, was thrilled to have another king actually send his family to visit him. He was so happy that someone of importance had made such an effort to come and see him that he decided to show the king's son and the men who accompanied him all his kingdom and all his treasures. Of course, pride had returned to Hezekiah, and he loved the attention and admiration from the visitors who were in awe over all that he had. In his naiveness and foolishness, Hezekiah enjoyed their complements and seeming friendliness.

When they left to return to the nation of Babylon, Isaiah the prophet came to visit Hezekiah again and asked him what he had said to these men. Hezekiah told Isaiah, with much pleasure and boasting, how he had shown the men of Babylon all his kingdom, all the treasures of his kingdom, and the treasures of the house of God. Isaiah then prophesied, with great disappointment and grief over Hezekiah's lack of discernment and discretion, that the days would come when Babylon would return and take all that Hezekiah had shown them—all that was in his house and in the kingdom, and all the treasures of the house of God. They would also take young people as well as some of Hezekiah's family as captives, and would ultimately destroy Judah.

Years later, the prophecy was fulfilled just as Isaiah had said. The Book of Daniel records that Daniel, Shadrach, Meshach, and Abednego were some of the young men taken to serve in Babylon, along with all the treasures of the kingdom.

You may say, "So what does this have to do with me?" The lesson to learn is when you seek the attention and admiration of others by displaying those valuable parts that should be kept protected and hidden, be warned that someone will eventually come along to steal those valuable items that you have revealed, and leave you with heartache and loss.

Fish Bait and Lures

Have you ever seen fishing lures or talked to fishermen about the different kinds of bait? In order to catch particular kinds of fish, fishermen use certain bait and lures to attract attention. If you want to catch a certain fish, you will use a particular lure.

Some lures are shiny, and others wiggle around to draw the fish to come after it. Curious fish go after the lure and get caught.

A girl or woman dressed in sexy clothes is just like that lure. If she exposes enough and moves herself around long enough, like the fish, a guy will come and take a bite.

Every girl and woman has treasures given to her by God. But if she thinks like Hezekiah that she hasn't attracted much attention and becomes over-anxious with the first visitors who come along and show some interest, she may foolishly show them some of her valuable possessions. And the more she shows, the more they learn about her and her possessions. The day will come when someone will find her in a vulnerable situation and steal her valuables. We will always pay a price when we show our treasures. It may not cost you the first day, but the day will come when you will have to pay.

Wake up and guard your treasures, guard your heart, and guard your life. Proverbs 4:23 says, *"Keep thy heart with all diligence….."* Verses 26 and 27 say, *"Ponder the path of thy feet, and let all thy ways be established* [by God's leading]. *Turn not to the right hand nor to the left: remove thy foot from evil."* Let Jesus be your Security Guard. Proverbs 3:6 says, *"In all thy ways acknowledge Him, and He shall direct thy paths."* Submit to Him so that He can bring your life into His divine order and leading. He will protect you from thieves. Proverbs also tells us that discretion will deliver you from the way of the evil man and from the man who speaks lies (see Prov. 2:11-12). You are precious to Jesus. He loves you and doesn't want you to be deceived. He values your life and wants you to fulfill His purposes for your life.

Thoughts to Remember

Here are some closing thoughts to remember:

1. Your physical body can be compared to valuable jewels. Just as people in the world guard their expensive jewelry, you should guard your body from possible thieves.

2. There are always costs and consequences to be paid when you show your treasures.

3. Guard your treasures, guard your heart, and guard your life. Let Jesus be your Security Guard! Listen to your heart because that is where Jesus speaks to you. Your heart will warn you if something might not be a good direction to take.

4. Lack of discernment and discretion can cause you to lose everything you have. Proverbs 2:11-12 says that discretion will deliver you from the evil man and from the man who speaks lies.

Chapter Nine

The Perfect Body

IT seems that everywhere you look, there are images (pictures) of women with perfect bodies—models, actresses, and other famous women on posters, TV, billboards, magazines, and life-size store advertisements. These images consume the mind of many girls and women to the point that they will do anything to look like them. Billions of dollars are spent annually on cosmetics, hair products, and clothing. Some girls and women become consumed with physical exercise and dieting. Some starve themselves. Others submit to plastic surgery, in order to have the perfect body.

These images all around us seem to say, "If you want to be happy or improve your self-image, you need to look like this picture. If you want lots of attention or if you really want to "go somewhere in life, you need to have a body like this movie star or that model, or the hair, makeup, and style of clothes they wear. Of course, these images are meant to entice you to spend time and money in order to become that image of "the perfect life." But it is a lie. As you strive for or even reach some of the goals these false images portray, you will never find the peace and happiness that only Jesus can give.

Magazines, TV sitcoms, and movies promote the idea that in order to have a great self-image and to be admired by others, a woman has to look "sexy" all her life. "Sexy" seems to be the focus and main concern of many girls and women. It seems that girls and women of all ages are driven to have a certain look because this is what the fashion world and the media says is the thing to do. I read in a *USA Today* newspaper article that movies such as *Stacy's Mom* portray a mom flaunting her body in a red bikini to show that she still has the stuff.

> A year and a half after this movie's release, the hit ditty by Fountains of Wayne, about a guy lusting after his girlfriend's mother, continues to strut through the airwaves...

> A Fresno California radio station sponsored a "hotmom contest"; listeners brought their moms to the studio and a "hottest mom" was crowned. The song served as the soundtrack to a Dr. Pepper ad, which features a mom emerging from a minivan to greet a clutch of boys (and dispense soda), the wind lifting up her shirttail ever so slightly.

> The song has "definitely taken on a life of its own," says Fountains of Wayne's Adam Schlesinger, who wrote *Stacy's Mom* and swears that, much to the dismay of teenage boys across the USA, she doesn't actually exist.

> Schlesinger acknowledges that he's paying homage to *The Graduate's* Mrs. Robinson, perhaps pop culture's most famous seductive matriarch.[1]

Being sexy-looking throughout life is very popular right now, keeping girls and women mentally, emotionally, and physically occupied. And yes, even Christian women don't want to be outdone by the world; they want to look sexy too. However, God gave sex for intimacy between a husband and wife. Looking sexy is for the marriage bedroom, not for public display. Christian women, like any other women, who crave looking sexy will attract men who only want them for sex.

Focusing on Eternity or Forfeiting Your Soul

It may surprise some people, but seduction spirits *do* go to church looking for other lusting spirits. While some Christians are beginning to speak up and say that *seductive* and *holy* just don't mix, many other Christians are compromising with a mixture of worldliness and God.

Let me ask you as a Christian girl or Christian woman, do you really want to be known in Heaven for being sexy and seductive on earth? When you stand before God to give an account for what you did with your life here on earth, will He be impressed with how "sexy-looking" you were, or will He ask you about things such as how you related His Gospel to other people?

Jesus said:

> ...*If any person wills to come after Me, let* [her] *deny* [herself] *[disown (herself), forget, lose sight of (herself) and (her) own interests, refuse and give up (herself)] and take up* [her] *cross daily and follow Me [cleave steadfastly to Me, conform wholly to My example in living and, if need be, in dying also]. For whoever would preserve* [her] *life and save it will lose and destroy it, but whoever loses* [her] *life for My sake,* [she] *will preserve and save it [from the penalty of eternal death]. For what does it profit a* [woman], *if* [she] *gains the whole world and ruins or forfeits (loses)* [herself]*? (Luke 9:23-25 AMP).*

This Scripture focuses on the fact that if you choose to be a follower of Jesus here on earth, you will have to deny yourself. I don't mean that you can't ever go shopping or that you should not exercise. What I mean is that these areas must be kept in submission and right priority under the attitude of "seeking the Kingdom of God first."

It's time to evaluate yourself. Everything in your life needs to be brought "under the microscope" of the lordship of Jesus. His lordship will help you live your life to the fullest potential that He wants for you, and He will help you to live for eternal purposes instead of being focused on yourself and your desires. This will keep you in the right mind-set. Instead of comparing yourself with others around you, you set your focus on obeying Him and allowing Him do what He wants to do with your life. This is freedom and fulfillment.

However, the enemy has devised a scheme to tempt the Christian to focus on being like, sounding like, looking like, and doing things like somebody else. How stressful! There is a constant barrage by the media of images of beautiful girls and women. Companies want you to compare yourself with these images and then buy their products in the pursuit of looking just like these pictures. These advertisements affect the church world as well. Christians observe the appearance of other Christians and then want to look like, sound like, dress like, and be just like them.

Many years ago, I fell into this comparison trap and was guilty of thinking I was inferior to other Christians around me. It seemed like I just didn't measure up. Then one morning I sat down to pray and read the Bible, and my Bible fell open to Second Corinthians 10:12: "*For we dare not make ourselves of the number, or compare ourselves with some that commend themselves: but they measuring themselves by themselves, and comparing themselves among themselves, **are not wise**"* (emphasis added). Wow! That Scripture jumped out at me that very moment. I knew God was speaking to me. I asked Him to forgive me for comparing myself and measuring myself to others.

Then I made a decision to simply live my life obeying His voice and measuring myself according to His Word.

I'll admit that there have been other times in my life that I was tempted to compare myself. Those kinds of thoughts can be depressing. But I came to understand that I cannot live the Christian life by my feelings—feelings can go up and down. We must live the Christian life by faith in what God says about us and refuse to allow comparison thoughts to rule us. The more I began to meditate and pray the Scriptures about who I am in Christ and His life in me, the greater my confidence grew and my self-image changed.

Physical Exercise

Does the Bible have anything to say about keeping ourselves physically fit? Yes. However, physical fitness involves more today than what it meant for people in Bible days. The only transportation then was riding a donkey, horse, or camel; and if you had the money to buy one, a wagon was available. Walking was a normal way of life. Food was prepared organically. Fast foods, preservatives, and modern technology were not in existence. Their main concern was making sure the water was safe to drink. There weren't a lot of choices when it came to eating and drinking. Life was very simple. It was harder and most activities took longer to accomplish.

Today, although modern technology has made life easier in some respects, it has also created a number of problems. We now have much more opportunity to indulge in unhealthy food and drinks, and because we have access to several modes of transportation, people suffer from lack of exercise. Consequently, more people are physically ill. Poor eating and drinking habits along with little or no physical exercise can even cause death.

First Timothy 4:8 says, *"Bodily exercise is all right..."* (TLB).

Paul says that physical exercise is okay. He doesn't say it's wrong or that it is a sin. He affirms that it is good for us. He understood the need for physical fitness because he referred to it and even compared athletes training to the Christian life in several letters that he wrote (see Heb. 12:1; 1 Cor. 9:24-27; Gal. 5:7.)

In First Corinthians 9:24-27, Paul states that when an Olympic runner prepares himself to run in a race in order to receive a prize, he has to strive or put effort into improving his running ability. An Olympic runner has to become temperate or self-controlled in *all* things. He establishes boundaries in his life regarding his time, his diet, his exercise, his rest, and his activities. He keeps his body under subjection. He exhibits self-restraint. He doesn't eat or drink anything he wants to, even when others around him are doing so. He is focused on running to the best of his potential for the prize.

Paul certainly walked a lot and had to have been physically fit to travel as much as he did and establish the churches that he did. He knew physical fitness enabled him to accomplish God's will.

Our society today needs physical exercise. The U.S. government actually stated a concern for Americans' physical well-being in the *USA Today* newspaper of January 2005 and then again later in the summer of 2005. Many doctors feel that major diseases could be reduced and avoided if more Americans would simply walk or jog thirty minutes to one hour, four or five times a week.

The word *exercise* means "to use; to practice; to exert your body and mind or faculties for improvement; to discipline oneself; to train; to use effort to improve."[2] In order to improve yourself, you must first have the desire to do so; otherwise, you will not make the effort that it takes to walk or jog. Some people wait until they are diagnosed with a serious disease before they make an effort to improve their well-being. Why wait until there is danger? Many times, it is too late.

Being concerned about physical fitness does not mean we're focusing on building a "perfect, sexy" body. Medical science tells us that physical exercise is good for our entire well-being. Even doctors of psychiatry realize that physical exercise such as walking or jogging helps people mentally and emotionally. When jogging or walking briskly, the brain releases endorphins. This actually sharpens a person's ability to think more clearly And I have found that it helps to reduce stress. Aerobic exercise causes the heart to pump correctly and helps clear arteries that lead to the heart, as well as strengthen the immune system. In addition, the organs that help cleanse our physical system are activated from physical exercise. Medical doctors agree that walking or jogging helps a person maintain healthy organs as well as avoid a lot of sugar buildup in the system.

My husband and I have had to make time to jog regularly. It isn't a legalistic thing. It is a discipline that we realize we need. If we miss some days, we don't give up or quit, we just start back again. We've come to understand that it is a habit that benefits us and we have to make time to do it.

I can remember the Holy Spirit prompting me to get out and walk or jog, and I knew I had to obey that voice inside of me. I'm amazed at how many Christians shove aside the promptings of the Holy Spirit when He tries to tell them commonsense things they need to do in order to avoid trouble later on. He will talk to you about your physical well-being just like He talks to you about your spiritual well-being, and it is to your benefit to listen to Him and obey Him.

Spiritual Exercise

In First Timothy 4:8, Paul says, *"Bodily exercise is all right, but **spiritual exercise is much more important** and is a tonic for all you do. So exercise yourself spiritually and practice* *being a better Christian because that will help you not only now in this life, but in the next life too*" (TLB, emphasis added). The previous verse says, "*Exercise thyself rather unto godliness*" (KJV). Paul states that while physical exercise profits us some, spiritual exercise has value for all things. Just as it takes effort to physically exercise, we also need to use effort to improve our spiritual lives in knowing God and in living a surrendered life. He encourages Christians to focus on exercising themselves to live a life that is godly and is a witness drawing others to Jesus.

Some think reading the Bible, praying daily, and attending church weekly are forms of legalism. On the contrary, these godly practices are necessary in order to stay spiritually healthy. These are disciplines that we need, just as we need to brush our teeth and take a shower each day for health and hygiene reasons—and believe me, other people appreciate you for practicing these forms of self-discipline. No one likes stinky bodies or smelly breath.

We all need self-discipline in our lives, including discipline to keep Jesus as the center of our focus, because we can very easily allow other things—even good things—to distract us, taking our time and attention.

When a Christian becomes spiritually depleted by not taking time to read the Word of God, pray, seek Him, go to church, and build godly friendships for accountability, that person will begin to live by her emotions (such as fear, anger, and lust) and her desires (or passions). And when a Christian lives by her emotions, she becomes a target for the enemy to deceive her into wrong thinking. Wrong thinking then produces wrong actions. The end result is heartbreak, loss, and pain, and sometimes self-destruction. When we think that attending church just once a week is enough, or when we neglect to renew our minds daily to the Word of God, we set ourselves up for deception.

When Paul wrote and told Timothy that he needed to encourage people to not only exercise physically but exercise themselves in godliness, he wanted them to understand that spiritual exercise is the priority. It's important not to get so focused on your physical body that your whole identity becomes wrapped up in your outer person rather than on your spiritual relationship with Jesus.

I know of a young Christian woman who weekly attended a strong church all her life. She married and had children. Over the years, she secured a good job and developed friendships, but she became focused on her physical appearance.

One day she was hurt in an accident that left her paralyzed on one side. Consequently, she struggled with her physical looks. Even though she was still beautiful, she felt ugly because she didn't have full use of her body on one side. Her family loved her, but because the image in her mind continued to torment her, she eventually committed suicide. In the note she left, she explained that she felt her family would be better off without her. Of course, this was not true; she had been deceived.

While many people become physically fit, they neglect to build up their lives spiritually. Yet, in seeking after the fantasy of a perfect body, they've come to find that dream to be an empty vessel. Jesus doesn't want us to lose sight of the most important goal in life—knowing Him more than we know Him now.

Anorexia and Bulimia

As we mentioned at the beginning of this chapter, television and other forms of media constantly bombard us with the message that we need to have the perfect body. These images consume the minds of some girls and women to the point that they will do anything to look like these images. Anorexia and bulimia have been two unfortunate results for which medical doctors have had to treat many. These sicknesses cause girls and women to waste away—some to the point of death.

Anorexia is a serious eating disorder where a girl stops eating because she thinks she is fat and fears weight gain. Bulimia is a disorder in which a girl experiences frequent and uncontrollable periods of overeating called "binges." After binging, most bulimics purge (eliminate) their food by forcing themselves to vomit or by taking large doses of laxatives to help empty the bowels, preventing them from gaining weight. Most bulimic girls don't realize the serious consequences of such actions, including the release of body acids that eat away at the enamel on their teeth.[3] Their organs can be damaged due to the unnatural things they have done to rid themselves of waste.

Many of these girls are convinced that they have things under control, but once again, they are deceived. Something else is controlling them. Most girls with these types of illnesses normally have to seek professional help to free themselves and live normally again. In many situations, their organs become so damaged that it causes them hardship for years.

Surgical Alternatives

Because of the high demand for the "perfect body" and the income that can be generated convincing women to keep searching for that perfect body, there are clinics all over the country where women can have their bodies surgically enhanced to their specifications. It's called "extreme makeover." A woman can have surgery on everything from a tummy tuck to breast and hip enlargement with silicone injections, or saline implants to shrinking the waistline, removing wrinkles with Botox injections, adding hair or removing hair, and enlarging or thinning lips. Some women have actually have the "Cher" (a Hollywood movie star) operation, getting the lowest rib removed so they can have smaller waistlines. The surgical list for achieving a perfect body is extensive. I wonder at times what God thinks about women trying to recreate themselves.

Even so-called family television shows promote surgery as a commonplace solution if you are dissatisfied with your physical appearance. One evening about 6:35 P.M. I turned on the TV to watch the news after coming home from work and eating supper. The news had just finished and a sitcom began, and I stood there for about five minutes. I don't know the name of the program, but it showed two ladies who were friends discussing an operation one of them was scheduled for. Then the husband walked in.

The wife revealed that she was scheduled for surgery to enlarge her breasts and her hips. There was laughter, then the husband said he liked her just the way she was. The friend said, "Uh-oh, here we go with male chauvinism." The wife then replied, "Now, you know that no one takes a second look at me when we walk into a restaurant, but when a woman has bigger breasts or a bigger bottom, all the men turn and look. I'm tired of not being noticed." Then in order to avoid an argument, her husband replied that she could do whatever she wanted to do.

I turned off the TV and thought to myself, *This married woman doesn't care what her husband thinks.* He was happy with the way she was. It wasn't about being attractive for her husband. It was about being noticed by and attractive to other men. *She lusted to be lusted for.* Women who strive for a perfect body in order to receive attention are just as guilty as men can be of the sin of lust.

This kind of television programming says to people, "You need to do whatever you want to do to fulfill your lust and get what you want." I was amazed that this was not some late-night sitcom; rather, it was early evening when children would be watching as well. It was forcing thoughts into people's minds that it's okay to do these things to make yourself happy in order to like yourself. What about learning to accept our lives as Jesus accepts us and as he created us and then simply walk in some self discipline in the areas we may need to improve.

The following is an excerpt from an article on FOXNEWS.COM, August 3, 2004. Some might think this woman has everything—the perfect body, public attention and awe, and the financial ability to get whatever she wants.

> LONDON (An interview with Halle Berry from the movie "Catwoman"): "Beauty? Let me tell you something—being thought of as a beautiful woman has spared me nothing in life," she said. "No heartache, no trouble. Love has been difficult. Beauty is essentially meaningless and it is always transitory." At a news conference to promote her movie, "Catwoman," the 35-year-old Berry criticized the obsession with beauty and youth that she said prompted some to get plastic surgery. "Personally, I'm really saddened by the way women mutilate their faces today in search of that," said Berry, who won an Oscar for "Monster's Ball." "There is this plastic, copycat look evolving and that's frightening to me....It's really insane and I feel sad that's what society is doing to women."

Wow! It sounds like Halle Berry has more understanding on this issue than a lot of Christian women do.

In *USA Today*, July 29, 2004, Robert Davis, in an article, "Teens' Cosmetic Dreams Don't Always Come True," wrote:

> In 2003, almost 336,000 teens 18 or younger had some kind of cosmetic surgery or procedure, a 50% increase over 2002.
>
> Patient-safety advocates believe that *many of the teens having surgery are unnecessarily putting themselves at*

risk of injury or even death. Teens face different obstacles in making a decision like this, experts say. They are often insecure and naïve about medical risks. And they literally are not always finished growing up.

Yet the number of girls 18 or younger having breast augmentation surgery is climbing—up 24% from 2002 to 2003. Parental consent is needed for patients under 18. There have been reports of girls getting breast implants as gifts for high school graduation.

Plastic surgery, like any surgery, can go wrong as it did for Kacey Long of Ennis, Texas, at age 19, who dreamed of looking like movie star Julia Roberts in her Oscar-winning 2000 portrayal of a famous office worker—Erin Brokovich.

Her decision was easy. A friend vouched for the surgeon. She could picture herself being happier after surgery. She had nearly half of the $4,500 cost, and the doctor agreed to take the rest in installments. So she became one of about 220,000 women who had breast augmentation surgery in 2001.

"I wish I had never done it," says now 22-year-old Long, who began feeling sick and weak within months after a plastic surgeon enlarged her breasts to size D. "I couldn't lift my arms. It disabled me within a year."

Although research has not proved that implants can cause serious diseases, Long says she has been diagnosed with systemic silicone poisoning from the shells surrounding the saline implants, rheumatoid arthritis, fibromyalgia and chronic fatigue syndrome.

She had the implants removed in September—a procedure that was documented for MTV's "I Want a Famous Face," which follows young plastic surgery patients.

Long says she feels lucky to be alive. "Every time you go under anesthesia, *you may not wake up.*" [That certainly is not encouraging.]

Long, who now has breasts that are slightly larger than her real breasts had been without implants, asks, "Why didn't my doctor tell me I was still growing?"

*Nobody tracks deaths or injuries caused by plastic surgery, but one study found that one in 50,000 liposuction surgery patients **die**.*

From May 2003 to January 2004, five people died in Florida after cosmetic surgery in New York this year; two women—one the wife of a cardiologist and the other Olivia Goldsmith, author of *The First Wives Club*—also died after cosmetic procedures. [Nobody talks about these facts.]

"The big problem with adolescents is they are being operated on at the most tumultuous time in their bodies. They may not recognize the permanence of what they're doing," says David Sarwer, a psychologist at the Center for Human Appearance at the University of Pennsylvania medical school.

Dennis Hurwitz, a plastic surgeon and clinical professor at the University of Pittsburgh, agrees.

"Plastic surgeons are operating psychiatrists," he says. "Good plastic surgeons talk to prospective patients to get to the root of *why* they want to change their looks," he says, which is especially important with teens. "It takes a lot of effort."

He says he convinces two-thirds of the teens who come to him seeking plastic surgery that they don't need to be changed. Teens risk making a decision they'll regret. Hurwitz says, "You must recognize their impulsive behavior."

One of his patients, Jennifer, had a bump removed from her nose at 18. Her nose was injured and her breathing impaired after a cheerleading accident. Now 20 and studying to be a pharmacist, she did not want her last name published to protect her privacy.

"It's a very traumatic experience," Jennifer says. "It should not be used for perfection. Society today views surgery as no big deal anymore. But this is not something to do just because you want your body to be perfect."

"You're not going to have too many plastic surgeons saying you don't really need this," says Diana Zuckerman, president of the National Center for Policy Research for Women & Families. *"Once you get in the door, of course, the doctors are saying everything they can to persuade you to have surgery."* [Remember, to them it's about making *money*.]

Zuckerman wants rules to protect girls from plastic surgery.

"Breast implants are not approved for anyone under 18, but any doctor can perform the surgery legally," she says. "I'd like to see the American Society of Plastic Surgeons have a policy saying we think our doctors shouldn't do this to anyone under 18."

Reality TV shows get some of the credit for America's love affair with plastic surgery. Millions of people have tuned in to Fox's "The Swan" and ABC's "Extreme Makeover" to watch what doctors call oversimplified and unrealistic transformations of average people.

Arthur Aaron Levin, director of the Center for Medical Consumers in New York, offers another ques-

tion for young patients to ask as they enter what he calls medicine's "uncharted waters" of medical errors: "Is it worth your life?" [Good question!] (emphasis added).

In an Internet article, "Government Studies Link Breast Implants to Cancer, Lung Diseases, and Suicide," by Diana Zuckerman, Ph.D., and Rachael Flynn, MPH, they state:

Two major studies raise questions about the long-term safety of breast implants. A team of researchers led by Louise Brinton, Ph.D., of the National Cancer Institute (NCI) recently published these studies on the long-term health effects of breast implants. *One of the studies found that women with breast implants are more likely to die from brain tumors, lung cancer, other respiratory diseases, and suicide compared to other plastic surgery patients. The other study found a 21% overall increased risk of cancer for women with implants, compared to women of the same age in the general population.* [Is anybody listening?]

While the authors were not able to determine whether implants caused these illnesses, the results show a doubling of brain cancer and a tripling of lung cancer, emphysema, and pneumonia for women with implants. Even though these findings were described as "unexpected," they are consistent with previous research that shows brain abnormalities and lung problems related to breast implants. *There was also a four-fold increase in suicide for breast implant patients, which seems to contradict the manufacturers' assertion that implants improve a woman's feeling of self-worth.* [All of you who want to feel better about yourself and you think you need surgery, think again. Surgery doesn't give you self-worth. Only Jesus can give you an understanding of your value, and He won't cause any negative side effects.]

Why are these results that we've mentioned so different from widely reported claims that breast implants do not cause any diseases? One reason may be that *the women included in the studies all had implants for at least eight years. Previous research included women who had only had breast implants for a year or two, or even a few months. Therefore, these new studies are the first to examine the long-term health effects of breast implants.* Unfortunately, even though diseases may take much longer than eight years to develop and be diagnosed, the findings from these well-designed studies indicate a potentially serious risk for the health of women with breast implants.

Another possible reason for this difference is that plastic surgeons and the implant manufacturers helped design and fund much of the previous research on implants; these groups have a tremendous financial stake—billions of dollars—in the outcome. Perhaps that is why so many previous studies focused on just a few rare diseases than a more comprehensive evaluation of the women's health... [Now we're getting to the real motive of doing cosmetic surgeries—money.]

Since approximately 2 million women in the United States already have breast implants and another 300,000 are planning on getting them this year, research on the long-term health effects is long overdue[4] (emphasis added).

Let me say that it is understood that when women have breast cancer and need to have a breast removed, reconstructive surgery becomes a necessity to look normal again. I believe God provides medical help for women in this condition. The motive for the surgery is not based upon lust, but is based upon continuing to function in their lives as before.

It is a disappointment, however, to realize that many church-going women, just like women of the world, want surgery to achieve a perfect body. What's wrong with this picture? Have some unconsciously made their bodies their priority instead of seeking to know Jesus more?

Evaluate Your Focus

We each have to ask ourselves, "What is my focus on? Is it on Jesus and getting to know Him more than I've known Him? Is it on reaching the lost or helping those around me in need?" It is obvious that operations to look sexier will not help us know Jesus more, reach the lost, or help others in need. If you say, "It's to keep my boyfriend or husband," then your boyfriend or husband and you probably need counseling—not surgery. A relationship based on physical appearances is shallow and will ultimately fall apart. Taking time to evaluate your life can help you see if your focus has become more on you than on God and others. Some questions you should ask yourself as a Christian are:

- Does Jesus want me to have surgery to have a "perfect body"? What is my motive for doing this?

- Is the motive of my heart pure or is it based on lust or even based on the fear of losing a relationship?

- Am I focusing more on my physical appearance than I am on what He wants me to use my time and thoughts for?

- Will getting surgery bring God more glory? Could it be just a selfish direction that I want to take?

- Am I so consumed with myself that I am unaware of what others think of my Christian example in the way I dress and how I emphasize my body?

- Do I care only about Christian friends who look like me and like to be "sexy-looking"? Or do I also take the time to consider relating with those who are poor, needy, crippled, deformed, retarded, old, smelly, sick, or bound in some way that others have no time for?

Take a moment to look around your life. If you surround yourself with only those people who look like you or are motivated in the same things you like to do, you will never experience true Christianity. Christians, like Jesus Christ, need to learn to relate to all kinds of people and share the gospel with them. Jesus needs "Jesus people" in this hour to reach people just like He did.

Perfect Images

Surrounded by *images* of physically perfect bodies and women who appear to be able to get anything they want and any man they want, we can be easily distracted from the real and meaningful purpose of life.

Images are "representations of a person or thing; a picture." The word *imagination* comes from the root word *image* and means "an image in the mind; it is the power of the mind that selects and forms ideas and thoughts by what has been seen, heard, or felt, causing a person to create in the mind something more than it really is."[5] Imagination isn't real. Good questions to ask include: Are the images of beautiful, happy, and perfect bodies really real? Are they really happy? Do they have a perfect life? Or are they still searching for true peace and joy? Are they contented and fulfilled? Or is someone creating images in order to convince you that these women are the happiest women in the world who have everything they want, because it means more money for them?

The truth is, many of these beautiful girls and women who are placed before the public are really hurting. Some are lonely; some are still searching for lasting love and happiness. Many of them need help that no one around them knows how to give. Some are drinking themselves to death. Some are taking drugs to survive. Some are anorexic and starving themselves to death Some have tried to fill their search for true love with one sexual relationship after another, and in doing so, they have severed all the good relationships they once had with those who sincerely cared about them. Some of these beautiful women have given up and in depression they have committed suicide. There are many who have reached the top of what the world calls success and the perfect sexy body but found it an empty, hopeless existence.

Images can consume our thinking. In the Old Testament, God warned Israel not to make for themselves images because He knew they would worship the images instead of Him. Remember, *worship is what consumes your thinking most of the time and what your life revolves around.* What do you worship? Everyone worships something, even if they don't physically bow down to it. Some worship fashion. Some worship sports and physical fitness. Some worship their occupation. Some worship just "being cool." The list goes on and on.

What you worship consumes your thinking, your time, your energy, and your finances. Fashion, sports, and physical fitness are not bad in themselves, but if they begin to consume your life, they become wrong. God wants your worship. He does not want you to be consumed with anything else that takes your love from Him.

Over and over in the Old Testament, you can read that when a king (or leader) didn't worship God, he had images built for the people to worship instead. If a godly king reigned next in line, he would command the people to pull down the images (or idols) so they could worship God alone. Today, many people continue to worship images or idols; the only difference is these images are made of paper or on a screen (magazines, catalogs, TV, etc.), whereas the Old Testament images were made of stone or wood.

When your value, self-esteem, identity, joy, and fulfillment are wrapped up in the size of your breasts or bottom, your thin waist, or your excellent muscle tone, then you have made your body an image or an idol. I heard a minister once say that an idol is "anything that you try to get your life, joy, and self-esteem from, that only God can give."

God is not against health and physical fitness. He is not against fashion within boundaries of godly character. However, within *all these areas, He wants to be the **center** of your focus so* that you live a holy life.

If you spend more time reading magazines, watching the latest movies, and keeping up with famous people in order to look like those people, and less time reading or meditating on the Word of God, then something else is your god and not God Himself. God said if you love Him and want to know Him, you will love His words and keep them. But without a daily time in God's Word, you won't know Him.

God speaks to us through His written Word and by His Holy Spirit, prompting us with His thoughts. The Bible tells us to attend to God's words and submit to His sayings, to keep them in the center of our heart because they are life to us, and they will benefit our physical and spiritual health (see Prov. 4:20-22).

God's Word can actually strengthen you physically and spiritually when you keep it as the focus of your life. When you value God's Word, God's Word will raise your self-image and eliminate the stress of trying to improve your self-image by striving for a perfect body.

"Selfism"

When a person becomes focused on her self-image, she can miss her purpose and God's plan for her life here on earth. I realize not all Christians are consumed with themselves, but there are those who are more committed and diligent to their daily physical workout, their diet, and maintaining their young appearance than they are committed to daily time with God, weekly church attendance, and developing relationships of accountability with godly friends to enhance their spiritual growth and maintain their spiritual hunger.

In our world today, one of the craftiest tools of the devil is busyness. Busyness can distract a person from her commitment to God, and she becomes consumed with herself. In addition, if satan can weaken a Christian so that she neglects her time with God, she will not develop her ability to discern and will become more susceptible to deception. Never underestimate the enemy's ability to seduce you at weak moments in your life. He wants to divert your main focus from what is on God's heart, who wants a relationship with you that compares with nothing else in the world. He doesn't want token "hellos." He wants intimate fellowship and time alone with you. He wants to work with you like a team working together every day. He wants to flow through you to others.

Even as a Christian, it's very easy to acquire a "selfism" mindset. Paul wrote in Second Timothy 3:2 that one of the signs of the last days would be people who are *"lovers of their own selves"* or self-centered.

When someone becomes focused on herself, she isn't thinking about pleasing God and helping others; she is thinking, *Do others see me as beautiful, attractive, or sexy, and how will this benefit me?* She begins to love herself so much that all her energy, thought life, conversation, and money are focused on her, while the Lord and others become less of a priority.

We have to ask ourselves, "Do I receive my self-esteem, joy, and fulfillment when I'm noticed for my cool clothes and my physical body?" Some people get their self-esteem, identity, and joy from driving a certain car, wearing a special brand of clothes, or hanging out with certain people. There's nothing wrong with having a car, wearing name brand clothes, or being with people, but if they become your identity and fulfillment, then it becomes wrong.

If we love how we look so much that we lose sensitivity to reach out to the less fortunate, the poor, or those whom the world calls uncool, unlovely, and unfashionable, we have moved our focus off Jesus and living for Him, and instead, we become focused on living for ourselves.

Whatever good that you do, always make sure your motive stays in the perimeter of sincere love for God and for others and not selfish ambition of looking good to be noticed.

Selfism includes loving ourselves so much that we are not willing to give up the part of ourselves that God wants. Some say, "But I thought I'm supposed to love myself." You are! Jesus says in Matthew 22:39 that you are to love your neighbor as you do yourself. But notice, the previous verses say that you are to love the Lord your God with all your heart and with all your soul and with all your mind. God should receive first place in your love. Your love for Him will then correctly direct you in how you love others and how you love yourself.

Healthy self-love is not selfish or self-focused. It exists in someone who has accepted herself for who God made her to be. She is not trying to be someone else. She is not struggling to get attention. She isn't thinking about herself when she reaches out to help someone else. She can bring healing and wholeness to others because she knows she is whole in Jesus Christ.

Finding Your Identity and Security in Christ

As time goes by, according to natural law, the physical body changes. However, getting older is difficult for some women to accept. Yet God created seasons of life just as He created seasons of a year. Each season is different and each season has its benefits. *"To every thing there is a season, and a time to every purpose under the heaven"* (Eccl. 3:1). *"He has made everything beautiful in its time..."* (Eccl. 3:11 ASV).

Growing older doesn't mean you have to look frumpy. You can look sharp and dress with style and class in every season of life while maintaining your Christian standards of godliness. Yet some Christian women become fearful of losing their value as they grow older because their focus is on themselves and not on the eternal.

We live in a society where many women want to stop the age clock and look like twenty year olds forever—sexy twenty year olds, as a matter of fact! However, as Christians, we should carefully consider and discern the views of the world around us in light of what God's Word says. Many Christians appear to be guided by the views of the world rather than what is characteristic of God's holy nature.

The *USA Today* newspaper of Thursday, January 27, 2005, included a front-page story entitled, "Mommy Hottest—No frumpy stereotypes here. Fun and sexy is in the house!" featuring moms, in their 40s and 50s, who want to look like they are in their 20s. They are working out at the gym, scheduling plastic surgery, wearing sexy clothes and shoes, and driving cool vehicles. Following is a segment of that article:

> "'Yummy mummies' we call them in Australia," says Anna Johnson, the author of *Three Black Skirts: All You Need to Survive.* "They have kitten heels, cleavage, and they don't cut their hair short." Johnson, 38 and pregnant

for the first time, hopes to follow the Prada-lined path blazed by sultry moms such as Uma Thurman. "You're handing your body and your life over to your baby, but you don't have to hand your style over to your baby." [Note: What about handing your life and style over to God?]

So as low-rise jeans have become the norm, as people have stopped blinking at the sight of a bare belly, the image of a mom in a miniskirt and lip gloss simply seems less scandalous.

Historically, though, motherhood has been about "not looking like you're on the market [I suppose she means 'meat market']," Johnson says. The net effect was to go from being "a Camaro to a Volvo." [Obviously, Johnson sees the need for women to look like they are on display at a meat market.]

The shrinking generation gap, including the fact that moms increasingly gravitate toward their daughters' closets and jewelry boxes, is "one of the biggest changes in consumer behavior in the past five years," says Marshal Cohen of the NPD Group, a market research firm….It has gotten so that sometimes daughters' tastes are more conservative than mothers'… [Whoa! That's scary.]

A generation unwilling to give up many of the trappings of youth, not just chic clothes. They want to listen to rock 'n' roll into retirement and splurge on the latest electronic gadgets. Abercrombie & Fitch might be marketed to teens and college kids, but Cohen points out that 45- to 50-year-olds are scooping up the trendy togs, too. Likewise, the Honda Element was designed for 25-year-olds, but 45-year-olds are buying the boxy cruiser "even more so."

"I haven't seen the guilt. I see the 'I deserve this,'" says Casas, who also is the national spokeswoman for the American Society for Aesthetic Plastic Surgery. "It's not an entitlement but almost a feeling of 'I'm worth it. I'm important enough.'" [Is "sexy looking" really about your worth as a woman? Could it be about your lust to be noticed and lusted for and not letting age stop lust?]

"There's a lot of competitive mommyhood right now," says Jane Buckingham, author of *The Modern Girls Guide to Life*.

There's no doubt that every person is valuable and important to God. Having a sexy body, however, will not ultimately fulfill you or keep you happy.

It's interesting that the writer of Ecclesiastes wrote that as a king he tried everything he wanted in order to find happiness, fulfillment, and meaning to life, and ended up realizing it was all empty in itself and vanity. His final conclusion was, "Fear God and obey His commandments...because God will judge us for everything we do, including every hidden thing, good or bad" (Eccl. 12:13-14, author's paraphrase).

Scripture teaches us to love God more than we love anything else and learn who we are in Christ, finding our identity and security in Him alone. Because Jesus' identity was in His Father God, He was secure and didn't have to wonder if others liked Him or not. This released Him to reach out beyond Himself and minister to others. They were then able to see God in Him.

When you become actively involved in ministering, discipling, and helping others, you won't be focused so much on whether or not you look like a carbon copy of a magazine model. The people you care for won't be concerned about your perfect figure. They are more concerned about what you are doing to help their lives as a result of your relationship with God.

Proverbs 31:30 says, *"Charm can be deceptive and beauty doesn't last, but a woman who fears and reverences God shall be greatly praised"* (TLB). While some are spending all their efforts to gain a "sexy-looking, perfect figure," this Scripture says that the woman who is most admired and praised is the woman who fears God and lives to honor Him, allowing Him to use her hands to reach out to others. God also needs older women to encourage and teach younger women how to walk out God's Word in their lives (see Titus 2:3-5).

It's helpful to realize that no woman can look exactly like another woman because God made each person uniquely different. Although we should be inspired to remain at a proper weight and to maintain healthy and self-disciplined habits, we do not have to live in frustration, always striving for, but never achieving the perfect body. While keeping yourself disciplined, be grateful for the life God has given you. Don't put yourself down. God created you in His image and likeness (see Gen. 1:26-27). Romans 9:20 says, *"Who are you to criticize God? Should the thing made say to the one who made it, 'Why have you made me like this?'"* (TLB).

The psalmist wrote, *"You made all the delicate, inner parts of my body, and knit them together in my mother's womb. Thank You for making me so wonderfully complex! It is amazing to think about. Your workmanship is marvelous—and how well I know it"* (Ps. 139:13-14 TLB).

God made you and placed you on earth to fulfill His purpose. If you will seek to know Him, He will show you these purposes at just the right time. Second Timothy 1:9 says, "[He] *hath saved us, and called us with an holy calling, not according to our works, but according to His own purpose and grace, which was given us in Christ Jesus before the world began."*

God has gifted you with His grace and ability. You are unique! There is no one else just like you. *"Having then gifts differing according to the grace that is given to us...*" (Rom. 12:6). "*We are His workmanship, created in Christ Jesus unto good works, which God hath before ordained that we should walk in them*" (Eph. 2:10). Be who you are! Don't try to be someone else! God made your body for His glory to be revealed in you. If you don't look like a magazine model, don't let it paralyze you. Your greatest purpose is to bring God honor and glory with your life. No matter what your occupation, He wants to reveal who He is to the people around you. Move on with God and His purposes for you.

Thoughts to Remember

Here are some closing thoughts to remember:

1. Believe what God says about you and don't compare yourself with others. God wants you to measure yourself by His Word (see 2 Cor. 10:12).

2. You can be so focused on physical fitness that you neglect spiritual fitness. Both physical and spiritual exercise and fitness should be brought into balance (see 1 Tim. 4:8).

3. Worship is what consumes your thinking most of the time and what your life revolves around. Every person worships something—fashion, sports, physical fitness, career, God, etc. Who or what is your focus of worship?

4. Your body becomes an idol when your value, self-esteem, identity, joy, and fulfillment are wrapped up in the size of your breasts, your thin waist, or your muscle tone.

5. God wants to be the center of your focus. When you love Him first, He will help you love yourself and others in a spiritually healthy way.

6. You can't afford to neglect reading the Word of God, praying, and seeking the Lord daily; going to church; and having godly friends who will hold you accountable.

7. Fulfillment and peace regarding your self-image will not come through plastic surgery or having an "extreme makeover." Girls and women who are fulfilled and have an inner peace and confidence are those who have surrendered to Jesus and understand He is the center of their focus.

8. Those who have considered surgery for attaining the perfect body need to first examine their motives for having surgery. Asking themselves the questions: Does Jesus want me to do this? Why am I doing this? Will this help me glorify Jesus more? Will this help bring others to Jesus?

9. Your greatest purpose on earth is not to have a perfect body, but to live for Jesus and bring Him glory and honor with your life.

Endnotes

1. "Fountains of Wayne Has One Splashy Mama," *USA Today*, January 27, 2005, 2D.

2. Noah Webster, *1828 American Dictionary of the English Language*.

3. World Book Encyclopedia, Volume 1A and 2B © 1990 World Book, Inc.

4. http://www.cpr4womenandfamilies.org/implantgov-stdy.html, Accessed 6/11/03. New studies are: (1) Brinton, LA, Lubin, JH, Burich, MC, Colton, T, and Hoover, RN. Morality Among Augmentation Mammoplasty Patients, Epidemiology 2001; 12:321-326. (2) Brinton, LA, Lubin, JH, Burich, MC, Colton, T, Brown, SL, and Hoover, RN. Cancer Risk at Sites Other Than the Breast Following Augmentation Mammoplasty. *Annals of Epidemiology* 2001; 11:248-256.

5. Noah Webster, *1828 American Dictionary of the English Language*.

Chapter Ten

Using Discretion

*D*ISCRETION is the "ability to avoid thoughts, attitudes, words, and actions which could lead to undesirable consequences."[1] Proverbs 2:11 says, *"Discretion shall preserve thee, understanding shall keep thee."* In order to be preserved or kept safe from danger, you must have discretion that comes from God. Proverbs indicates that when we seek to know God, to increase knowledge of His Word and understanding, we will receive discretion.

Discretion is an awareness and sensitivity from God that guides us to do the right thing. But because of immaturity, young girls do not always have discretion. As they grow older, life experiences can be hard teachers.

Learning When You're Young

I remember a beautiful young teenage girl who had been raised in a Christian home and in church. She developed physically very early; at age 13 she looked like she was 16 or 17 years old. A rich young guy from another school met her at a public swimming area and was captured by her beautiful body in a two-piece bathing suit.

Because they were not old enough to date, they would meet at places to see each other. He had plenty of money so he bought her all kinds of gifts and treated her royally. Over a period of time, he began to make his moves with her sexually, and she became pregnant. He immediately suggested an abortion. However, while planning to carry it out, she decided it was wrong and couldn't go through with it. They told their parents, and when his parents found out that she did not want an abortion, they cut off all relationship with the girl because they didn't want their son's name to be tarnished. Within two weeks, the boy had another girlfriend and never had anything to do with this girl again. The girl's parents, loved her and supported her having the baby and helped her care for the baby afterward.

Four more years of high school was not easy, but she finished and graduated, though she was not able to do a lot of things other teenagers were free to do. She had to face rejection, loneliness, and responsibility at an early age. Although it was difficult she make it through that time. So, how important is it to learn discretion while you're young? It can spare a girl from a lot of heartache and pain.

Not only do you need discretion to avoid wrong and sinful circumstances and actions that will cause heartache and trouble, but discretion will also help you do what is right so you don't cause other people to have wrong thoughts and attitudes, or say and do the wrong things.

A few years ago, a group of teenage boys, while at our home, discussed who they felt were spiritual leaders in their school. When I asked about a certain girl, they looked at each other and then at me, and said, "She's hard to figure out. She sends mixed signals. When she's in a chapel service, she lifts her hands to God and enters into worship; but she dresses in a way that is sexy, and it makes a guy think that she wants him to come after her. She definitely doesn't dress modestly."

I was amazed that these young guys actually understood and spoke from a mature standpoint regarding the issue of girls' clothes and sending "mixed signals." This girl probably didn't understand discretion, which is no surprise, because her mother did not dress discreetly either. I've seen Christian moms bringing their kids to school or picking them up who wear clothes that definitely are designed to make guys turn and look at them. One husband who had had a struggle with pornography in years past, told his wife that she would have to take the kids to school because he did not want to have to look at moms dressed in tight revealing workout outfits who dropped their kids off at the same time. Discretion is something that a parent has to help their daughter understand and set an example for them to follow.

The Value of Modesty

Proverbs 11:22 says, *"A beautiful woman lacking discretion and modesty is like a fine gold ring in a pig's snout"* (TLB). In this Scripture, God is not calling anyone a pig; He is simply stating that a pig doesn't have any understanding of how to value what is precious. If you were to give a pig a bath and put a gold ring in its snout, it would still act like a pig. If the pig found a mud hole, he would go for it—gold ring and all, because the gold ring has no value to him. Even if he lost the ring, it would not bother him.

On the other hand, a gold ring and a beautiful woman who values that ring, fit together. Others around her admire it too. The gold ring in this example is symbolic of modesty or guarding your sexuality. When the beautiful woman lacks discretion and doesn't value her modesty, it is though she doesn't value a gold ring. If she gives up modesty and publicly wears sexy-looking, tight-fitting clothes with low necklines to reveal breast cleavage, miniskirts, see-through blouses, and low-slung pants to show her navel and draw attention to her body, she's just like the pig with a gold ring in its nose. She has no understanding of her value, and she lacks discretion that would help her understand the value of what is precious and protect it.

Honoring the One You Love

When we *"put ... on the Lord Jesus Christ"* (Rom. 13:14), we represent Him. In fact, First Corinthians 6:19-20 says:

*Haven't you yet learned that your body is the home of the Holy Spirit God gave you, and that He lives within you? Your own body does not belong to you. For God has bought you with a great price. **So use every part of your body to give glory back to God, because He owns it*** (TLB, emphasis added).

According to this Scripture, our body is God's house, and we must decorate it in submission to the One who lives within us. We consider Him in all things (see Heb. 12:1-3). Discretion will cause you to think about honoring Jesus. It will cause you to consider, "What would Jesus think about this?" Isaiah 28:26 says, *"For his God doth instruct him to discretion, and doth teach him."* He will teach and instruct us, but only if we allow Him to; then we must do what He wants us to do.

I remember when my husband and I were engaged to be married, I thought a lot about what he thought about me. I wanted to please him because I wanted to marry him. Our relationship to Jesus should be like finding our true love. Remember, love motivates you to please the one you love. Loving Jesus guides us when it comes to what we wear, where we go, what we do, and what we say. This is what is called "the fear of the Lord," which means loving God so much that you want to please Him and bring Him honor in every area of your life. You think about how

He feels about the choices and decisions you make. Knowing that He is holy (see 1 Pet. 1:13-17), you want to be holy in all your lifestyle (see 1 Tim. 1:9; 1 Thess. 4:7).

This kind of commitment causes you to be different than others who have not come to this point in their understanding of the Christian walk. Many think they want to be Christians because their friends are Christians; however, when it comes to changing their ways in honor and love for the Lord, their lack of commitment is revealed. *Commitment will always reveal true love. Commitment and true love will always require change.*

A Separate Life

Don't be teamed with those who do not love the Lord, for what do the people of God have in common with the people of sin? How can light live with darkness?

And what harmony can there be between Christ and the devil? How can a Christian be a partner with one who doesn't believe? And what union can there be between God's temple and idols? For you are God's temple, the home of the living God, and God has said of you, "I will live in them and walk among them, and I will be their God and they shall be My people." That is why the Lord has said, "Leave them [the world's way of thinking and those living by the world's standard]; *separate yourselves from them.* [This doesn't mean you have to withdraw from everyone around you. You do need Christians who love God around your life but you still live in this world. It means to live in a different way than the world around you lives (separated unto God). And if they do things or go places that are wrong, don't go along with them. They must see a difference in you if you belong to Jesus.] *Don't touch their filthy things, and I will welcome you, and be a Father to you, and you will be My sons and daughters"* (2 Corinthians 6:14-18 TLB).

Second Corinthians 7:1 says,

Having such great promises as these, dear friends, let us turn away from everything wrong, whether of body or spirit, and purify ourselves, living in the wholesome fear of God, giving ourselves to Him alone (TLB).

Over the years in ministry, many women have come to me for prayer who have experienced the pain and heartache of sin and wrong relationships. These women are ready to do whatever it takes, not only to be saved but to live in newness of life. They want the fear of the Lord and they want the truth. They don't mind being corrected and instructed in righteousness because they have experienced the "wages" or results of sin. Past experiences of heartache and pain due to a lack of discretion can create a greater awareness of what and what not to do in the future.

When these girls come out of the bar scene or prostitution, and are truly saved, they know they can never go back to that realm of life again. They've endured some hard and painful lessons, yet these life experiences have given them insight and a stronger sense of discerning deceptive people and seducers. They know that working a regular job may not pay much money, but they would rather be free inside. Immediately they want their lives to be brought into spiritual order.

I remember one young woman who had made a lot of money dancing at a bar. After making a commitment to Jesus, she changed jobs and was struggling financially and needed to pay her bills. Sometime later, she ran into the bar owner who offered her former job to her and said she could start that week. She told me that she went home and got out her little outfit from the closet and laid it on the bed. As she looked at it, she fell down on her knees beside the bed crying. She knew that she had made a commitment to God, and at that moment she felt God's grace rise up within her to say "no" to the owner. She then called him to inform him that she could not take the job.

Although it was difficult during that time, she kept her commitment to Jesus. Believe me, you will be tested on your commitment. At these times of testing, Jesus finds out whether or not you really love Him the most. It's called "laying down your life." Those who do, will find more and more that discretion will guide them. When you think more about what He thinks than what others think, discretion will guide you.

The Company You Keep and the Places You Go

Unfortunately, even young ladies from Christian homes say and do foolish things because they are influenced by the media and by a poor choice of friends. First Corinthians 15:33 tells us that wrong associations or bad company will corrupt or ruin good morals and good character in a person. Your discretion ability is affected by the people you hang around. Proverbs 13:20 says if you walk with wise people, choosing them as your companions, you will grow wise yourself. But if you keep company with fools, you will suffer and experience harm (see Prov. 13:20 The Jerusalem Bible).

You must use discernment regarding your choice of friends, because you become like those whom you associate with. Make sure they are not "clueless" or naïve. Also, make sure they have the same moral and godly values that you live by.

Some Christians adjust their values and beliefs to the values and beliefs of the friends they associate with because they want to be accepted by those friends. They are afraid to be different. It's called peer pressure. Compromise doesn't happen immediately. Normally, people hang around others who do wrong things that they tolerate over a period of time until finally their toleration moves to accepting the wrong things as okay. Following Jesus is not always easy; there are times when you will need to take a stand and be different from those around you.

In talking to a friend who is single and works for a Christian tour company that schedules trips to historical sites on the East coast, she shared with me that many of the Christian teenagers, ministers' kids, and young Christian adults in the groups want to go to ungodly places during their free time.

When most of the groups were given free time to shop, the girls wanted to shop at Victoria's Secret lingerie store to buy the latest sexy underwear. Her comment was, "I'm a single adult woman, but I don't even go to this lingerie store to shop because the lingerie is so focused on being sexy." Then she said, "I don't need to be thinking about being sexy when I am not married. I want the right Christian man to come into my life not wrapped up in sexual lust but in wanting to please God like I want to please God. Then the sexual part will go in the right direction."

Why are young Christian teens so concerned with having sexy, revealing underwear when they are not married? Is there no one teaching them a sense of discretion? Or could it be they are being swept into the world's view through the media's influence? My next question is, who sees what they are wearing? If they are so concerned about their underwear looking cool and sexy, could it mean that they are showing it to some guy they want?

Another place these teens went was to the MTV studio—definitely not a place that promotes modesty or a holy lifestyle. It seems odd that they want to bear the name "Christian," but want to live a life totally opposite of Christianity. Some identify with being a Christian like it's a fad. However, identifying with Jesus Christ is about giving up your life and the temptation of this world system in order to follow Him all your life.

Compromise—A No-Win Situation

Are you easily swayed by the crowd around you? Or are you strong enough to not go along with the crowd when you know something isn't right? Are you like a chameleon who changes with the setting.

Some Christian kids have learned to do the right things and say the right things in one setting, but then change in another setting like the chameleon lizard changes colors according to its environment. Do you think the same and act the same in every setting that you find yourself in? Are you always making an effort to be discreet in how you dress and how you come across to guys? Or would you rather compromise than practice discretion?

Warning: *Whatever you are willing to compromise, you'll eventually lose. Compromise* is a "concession to something derogatory where someone concedes and they accept what they are told as true, valid, or accurate. They yield to it."[2] *Once you start compromising, it is very difficult to stop.* Jesus called it "salt losing its savour" (see Matt. 5:13). Once salt loses its savour, it is *"good for nothing, but to be cast out, and to be trodden under foot of men."* Whoa! Those are strong words. Science has said that salt is one of the most stable compounds in the earth, but it can lose its savour two ways: (1) if it is mixed, contaminated, or diluted with another substance; and (2) if it is left out and exposed to the elements of weather, such as rain, snow, and heat.

Spiritually speaking, if you allow the world's way of thinking to cause you to compromise your convictions in order to be accepted, you have become a mixture, or diluted with another substance, and you have lost your savour. Or if you give into the seductions of the world's media, over a period of time you will lose your savour as a Christian. Exposing yourself to immorality, nudity, sex, and profanity, by watching the media, will gradually break down your own reasoning about modesty, and you'll begin to view things from a more liberal, worldly, immoral view. *It has been proven that we eventually accept what we tolerate over a period of time.*

When a Christian lives her life in a mixture, she develops very little discretion. Her discernment becomes clouded and she accepts what others do, whether right or wrong. So, in order not to compromise and in order to remain the salt of the earth that Jesus said we're to be, we have to make decisions daily to submit to God's written Word and to His Holy Spirit's conviction.

God's Word gives us knowledge of His will and His way of thinking. It is the wisdom of God. Those who want discretion also want knowledge and wisdom. Proverbs 2:10-11 says, "*When wisdom entereth into thine heart, and knowledge is pleasant unto thy soul; discretion shall preserve thee, understanding shall keep thee.*" Discretion causes a person to consider the outcome of her decisions and choices before acting them out, thereby avoiding trouble. When you take time to read, study, and memorize God's Word, you will choose to do the right thing. James 1:22 says if you hear God's Word taught or preached, but you don't *do* what the Word says, you deceive yourself. Some Christians acquire a little knowledge of God's Word, but they convince themselves they don't need to seek God daily. Then they start shoving aside the still small voice of the Holy Spirit. All of this leads to trouble.

Some have even gone to Bible school, but they still compromise, thinking they can walk in God's will while continuing to lust after things of the world. Jesus' lordship requires us to die to the lust of the flesh and live within boundaries so that lust can no longer have its way. In this position, we become sensitive to God's voice, more discreet in our actions, and more discerning of ourselves, of others, and of situations we face.

I realize living for Christ and dying to ourselves may sound extreme—but that's good. *Extreme* means to go to the farthest point; to press oneself to the utmost even if by great difficulty. It is setting our will to do whatever it takes to submit to God's will and not compromise. Unfortunately, many Christians struggle because they never press beyond what everyone around them is doing. They conform to the crowd and live in apathy. Extreme Christianity is passionate.

True Christianity is laying down your life for Jesus, which requires death to yourself and being raised to walk in newness of life (see Rom. 6:4). Paul even went on to say in First Corinthians 15:31b, "*I die daily*" (to the world, to himself, and to the flesh). That's surrender. God wants you to take heed to Paul's example and commit to Jesus Christ, identifying yourself as a Christian and surrendering as well.

Thoughts to Remember

Here are some closing thoughts to remember:

1. *Discretion* is the "ability to avoid thoughts, attitudes, words, and actions which could lead to undesirable consequences." Discretion will cause you to think about honoring Jesus. Discretion will cause you to consider the outcome of your decisions and choices before acting on them. Discretion will deliver you from evil (see Prov. 2:10-12). Discretion will cause you to want knowledge and wisdom.

2. Scripture compares a beautiful woman who lacks discretion and modesty to a gold ring in a pig's snout (see Prov. 11:22 TLB.) They don't go together. Your beauty is a treasure and you are valuable. Discretion will help you protect yourself from being hurt or misused.

3. Lack of emotion or passion toward God reveals an attitude of apathy. Apathy breeds compromise. Apathy is more concerned with going along with the crowd than standing up for what's right.

4. Do you compromise? Warning: Whatever you are willing to compromise, you'll eventually lose.

5. You eventually accept what you tolerate over a period of time.

6. Extreme Christians do not compromise. They are willing to go to the farthest point, even when difficult, in order to walk out God's will.

Endnotes

1. Bill Gothard, *Basic Youth Conflicts*.

2. *Merriam-Webster's Collegiate Dictionary, Tenth Ed.* (Springfield, MA: Merriam-Webster, Inc., 1996), 237-238.

Chapter Eleven

Dresses or Pants?
Is There a Problem?

S OMETIMES when discussing the subject of modesty, I've been questioned about women wearing pants. Although this is not an issue with everyone, it has been a concern of some. For centuries, the custom of dress for women has been dresses and skirts. The 1960s brought a change when the fashion industry began to promote pants as suitable clothing for women. Subsequently, some religious groups challenged this change, declaring it unscriptural, and used Deuteronomy 5:22 to support their belief.

Deuteronomy 22:5 states, "*A woman shall not wear man's clothing, nor shall a man put on a woman's clothing; for whoever does these things is an abomination to the Lord your God*" (NASB). The end of this verse in the New International Version says, "*For the Lord your God detests anyone who does this.*" In this Scripture, God says that a woman should not wear "man's clothing"; it says nothing about pants.

This may be enlightening to some—the men in Bible times *did not wear pants*. Even today when you travel to some nations of the world, men still hold to their cultural customs of wearing long dresses or robes as their daily garments. Early Church history reveals that men wore long flowing dresses and robes. There was a difference, however, in the men's dresses and the women's dresses to clearly identify male from female. And today, women's pants are clearly differentiated from men's pants.

Dress According to Your Sexual Identity

I remember several years ago, two women who had been delivered from the lesbian lifestyle and had completed Bible school, came to church one night dressed in trousers and oxford shirts. Because I had been in a position of discipling them, I had the opportunity and obligation to speak to them regarding what they were wearing. When I asked, "Why are you wearing that?" they laughed and said, "What do you mean?" I replied, "You know what I mean," as I pointed to their clothes. They said, "You don't miss a thing, do you?" I said, "Well, knowing that you've walked free from your former lifestyle, *discretion* should tell you that you can never wear trousers and dress manly again." They agreed.

So what did God mean in Deuteronomy 22:5? He meant that women are to wear clothes that people know are made for women, and men are to wear clothes that people recognize are for men. Otherwise, people will wonder whether they are homosexuals or lesbians. Anything that might identify you with lesbianism or homosexuality should be avoided. People know the clothes, the jewelry, and the mannerisms that characterize a person as homosexual.

According to Scripture, homosexuality and lesbianism are abominations to God (see Lev. 20:13, 18:22; Gen. 19:5 and Jude vs. 7 TLB). Sexual perversion, sodomy, homosexuality, orgies, bestiality, fornication, adultery, and incest were major reasons why Sodom and Gomorrah were destroyed. In the New Testament, Paul addresses the subjects again as sin (see Rom. 1:24-32; 1 Cor. 6:9-10).

The main point of Deuteronomy 22:5 is, women should not dress in a way that makes them look like a lesbian and men are not to dress in a way that makes them look like a homosexual. If we say that women cannot wear pants today because they didn't wear them in Bible times, then we would also need to say that men should not wear pants because neither did they wear them in Bible times. The issue is not pants; rather, men need to wear men's clothing, and women need to wear women's clothing.

My husband and sons would not wear the style of pants or pantsuits that my daughters and I wear. Our pants and pantsuits are made to look feminine. Likewise, we do not wear men's trousers or pants. There is a definite manliness in men's suits and men's trousers or pants.

I remember a young man who had come from another city to Tulsa years ago and gave his heart to Jesus, leaving the homosexual lifestyle and the occult behind. He moved into a home with a Christian couple in our church. For a year or so, it seemed he was doing well and becoming the man of God he was called to be. However, one day he announced he just couldn't live the Christian life anymore. He left the home he was in and returned to his former lifestyle of homosexuality.

One day as I was shopping in a department store, he walked up to me, wearing a dress and heels, with long hair and makeup. (Homosexuality has become so blatant today that people feel no shame or embarrassment and no need to hide their sin.) He asked if I recognized him, and I said yes and called him by his name. He replied, "Please don't call me that name anymore because I've changed my name to Barbie." Then he said he wanted to introduce me to his male fiancé.

I invited him to come back to church. He said, "Oh, they wouldn't accept me dressed like I am now." I told him we would accept him but that God would require him to change in his direction of clothes. I lovingly told him that no matter what he did to himself, he would always be a male. God created him a male, not a female. He only needed to repent, turn away from the sins of homosexuality and rebellion, and turn back to God and he would still be able to receive forgiveness. We were cordial with each other and then went our separate ways. I've not seen him since that time. I pray that he has repented.

However, where there is no repentance for sin, there will surely be a penalty. Even though many people may accept homosexuality as a normal lifestyle and even condone it, that doesn't make it acceptable to God. All sin has a payday. Those who continue in homosexuality will ultimately face a judgment time if there is no repentance. And understand that delayed judgment does not mean no judgment. Sin has its own judgment. It's a matter of sowing and reaping. When you sow to the flesh's desires, you will reap corruption.

Those caught in this trap of sin know deep inside that it is wrong. The good news is, as long as we have breath in our bodies, we have the opportunity to repent and receive God's mercy. We have come to know of many who have been healed and delivered from homosexuality. Today they are living whole lives and have families who are strong. I pray for an awakening in our country before it is too late and before many suffer eternal damnation (see Rom. 1:18-32; Rev. 21:8).

Inappropriate Pants and Shorts

Pants are now an accepted and suitable part of clothing for women in many Christian circles, but that does not constitute wearing pants that look as if you have been poured into them. Even though the world says to show what you've got or to flaunt the body God gave you, we have to ask ourselves, "*How does Jesus feel about the pants I'm wearing?*"

The tight, low-waisted pants that show your belly, your belly button, and the top of the back of your underwear don't communicate that you're dressing to please Jesus. Some people say, "I should be able to wear what I want. I can't help it if guys have a lust problem." Again, I ask, who is lusting who?

We live in a hedonistic and rebellious society where people want freedom to do whatever they feel like doing. I remember a few years ago hearing about a popular song entitled, "Nasty, Put Some Clothes On." Just the title of the song seems to say what is needed. If a Christian girl or woman dresses seductively, how can she expect the world around her to respect and honor what she has to say?

We have to ask ourselves, "What does God's Word say?" Jesus needs witnesses more than ever right now. He needs Christians (meaning "little Christs") to take a stand all the way for Him. That means what we do, what we say, and what we wear are to glorify Jesus with whom we identify.

Next, you may ask the question, "What about shorts?" When it comes to sports activities and the hot summer, shorts are an acceptable fashion. There are short shorts and there are longer shorts. There are tight shorts and loose shorts. As a Christian, listen to that small voice within your heart. That's the Holy Spirit. He will lead you not to wear anything that would create too much attention to your front and back bottom.

When you are wearing shorts, are people's eyes drawn to look at your body? When you are out jogging or running, does what you wear draw attention to your breasts? Through the years, my family and I have jogged for exercise. If we jog on a public jogging trail, many times the men in our family have to turn their heads and look another direction when meeting an oncoming female jogger simply because of what she is showing. The other day, I saw a girl jogging with just a small sports bra on and low-cut short shorts emphasizing her nice slender tan torso.

It's still fashionable to put on a T-shirt over a sports bra. It's also modest.

Modesty Reflects the Light

Matthew 6:22 says, *"The light of the body is the eye...."* As Christians, it should be our eyes that people focus on, not our body. If our eye is single (or pure and clear), then our whole body will be full of light. But if our eye is evil (if there is any impurity in our motives, or if we choose to live with no regard of others), then our whole body will be full of darkness.

The Word goes on to say that if the light that is in you be darkness (blinded by the seducing spirits of this world), how great is that darkness! We determine to keep our lives in the light by choosing to live within the boundaries of modesty in the way we wear pants or shorts. The way we wear our clothes reflects who we are following—Jesus or the world.

Thoughts to Remember

Here are some closing thoughts to remember:

1. God has no issue with women wearing pants. The issue is, men need to wear men's clothing and women need to wear women's clothing.

2. In Deuteronomy 22:5, God is referring to homosexuality and lesbianism. These are abominations to God. We are to dress according to our sexual identity as women (see Rom. 1:24-32; 1 Cor. 6:9-10).

3. Ask yourself, "How does Jesus feel about what I am wearing?" The way we wear our clothes reflects who

we are following. We are either followers of the world or followers of Jesus.

4. If dressed seductively, how can a Christian girl or woman expect the world to respect and honor what she has to say?

5. *"The light of the body is the eye..."* (Matt. 6:22). If our eye (our thoughts and motives) is single (pure) than our whole body will be full of light. But if our eye is evil (our thoughts and motives are impure or have no regard for how we are wrongly affecting others) than our whole body will be full of darkness. Are people able to focus on your eyes or are they distracted by how you are dressed so that they focus on your body?

6. The way we wear our clothes reflects who we are following—Jesus or the world.

Chapter Twelve

Who's Seducing Who?

*But the [Holy] Spirit distinctly and expressly declares that in latter times some will turn away from the faith, giving attention to **deluding and seducing spirits** and doctrines that demons teach* (1 Timothy 4:1 AMP, emphasis added).

WEBSTER defines *seduce* as to "draw aside or entice from the path of moral rectitude (or moral conduct of what is right) and duty (moral obedience and submission to God)."[1] *Seduction* is "being apt to mislead by flattering appearances and deception." Webster indicates that a seducing person is base enough (or low enough) that she could turn against another person, betray that person, and feel no conviction about what she does. A seducing person is "someone who tends to draw someone aside or entice from the path of moral rightness or standard of right; to entice to surrender chastity."[2] *Chastity* means "purity of body; freedom from unlawful intercourse of sexes; fidelity to the marriage bed; purity in words and phrases."[3]

A Desire to Be Pure

A woman (or a man) who is above flattery is least liable to be seduced, but the best safeguard is loving purity and holiness, and having a fear of the Lord with reverence to His commands.

Flattery is different than a compliment in that a *compliment* has no ulterior motive except to esteem and encourage another person. *Flattery* esteems and praises another person for personal benefit. Flattery will go as far as lying, in order to benefit from the person they flatter. Seductive people understand flattery. Their motives are never pure.

When you love purity, your heart will be disturbed when someone comes after you with impure motives. He may seem sweet and convince you that he is a Christian. He may even try to be helpful to you, but your spirit questions him and senses a caution. This is why you need a daily time in God's Word. God's Word is pure and your obedience to His Word purifies your soul (see 1 Pet. 1:22). God's Word also sharpens your discernment ability (see Heb. 4:12); however, an apathetic attitude toward God's Word will result in a vulnerability within you wherein you will become more easily deceived and seduced. When you love purity, you will have a respect for God's commands. You will discern deceptiveness and seduction when you face it. Not only could someone attempt to seduce you, but realize that that you as a female could be seductive in how you relate to guys.

Having a person to hold you accountable is an important factor in helping you recognize and turn from seduction. However, when you allow another Christian to have this kind of relationship with you, it will require humility on your part. You need someone who can be totally open and honest with you and who care enough about you to protect you from wrong directions. This needs to be someone who can examine your actions, choices, motives, and thinking.

Seduction Is a Spirit

According to First Timothy 4:1, *seduction* is a spirit. As Christians, we have received the Holy Spirit, but Paul warns us that there are demonic spirits battling against us, trying to influence our minds and emotions, our desires, and our will. This is an area of your soul. Your spirit is where the Holy Spirit lives, whereas your soul includes your desires, your emotions, your will, and your reasoning. It must be brought into submission and kept in submission to your spirit. The more we continue in God's Word and prayer, avoiding any situation that would create lust, and staying accountable to a true friend, the stronger our spirit becomes to resist and overcome the influence of seducing spirits.

Your eyes and ears are the entry gates to your soul. Guard them! Realize that if you watch people on TV or movies who seduce people, your soul is learning how seduction operates.

The media constantly advertises images to seduce, distract, and pull Christians into its way of thinking. Seducing spirits want to use Christian women to be seductive and convinces women that they need to attract attention. Satan (the champion seducer and deceiver) understands the power of persuasion that women have. After all, he seduced Eve and she then seduced Adam, and that's how lust and sin changed the world.

Body Language

Studies show that we communicate not only with our words but also with our bodies. We all know that "there is a look…and then there is a look." Remember when you were young and your mom or someone in authority gave you a look of disapproval when you had done something wrong? Even without saying a word, their body language said it all and you knew you were in trouble.

Many girls learn that they can get anything they want if they just look a certain way. Sometimes it's a look that says "pity me" other times it's a look that says "I'll give you what you want, if you give me what I want." Body language goes on all around us daily.

Sometimes when there is a need for more attention, a girl or woman will go to drastic measures. Sometimes when a woman loses weight she begins to wear clothes to reveal her new figure. She wants to show off certain parts of her body that she now feels proud of. The attention of people around her feels good.

If a woman begins to feed on the need for attention to her physical body, it's possible to give access to a seducing spirit that will influence and deceive her. One moment a woman can appear as sweet and innocent as can be, but then, all of a sudden, she begins to position herself in the pathway of a man she wants attention from. Walk with a certain move of the hips, flash a look of desire with her eyes and a smile that says, "I want your attention. Are you interested in me?" At another time, she might slide into a chair, flip her hair with her hand, slowly cross her legs when sitting down while purposely revealing enough leg to draw a man's eyes to look. Then slowly and purposefully lick her lips as she looks at or speaks to the man, hanging her hair across her eyes to create a seductive mystery about her face.

If a young girl learns the power of her sexual persuasion early enough and how it can be used to help her get her way, she can become controlled by a seducing spirit for years. It becomes a lifestyle and a way of manipulating others.

I remember years ago a woman came to our church, who used her eyes to seduce men. Some might call them "cat eyes." Most of the time she didn't have them fully opened, but instead she kept them in a relaxed, somewhat sleepy look as she talked with men. She would slowly bat her eyelids a few times during a conversation when men were present. The amazing thing was, when she talked with me alone, she kept her eyes normal and wide open. Several of the men on staff told their wives to communicate for them with this woman because they felt uneasy talking to her. She eventually left the church. She couldn't get attention from those she wanted it from.

A Flirt or a Friend

Another woman who attended our church years ago and liked to wear tight clothes, seemed to make every effort to be friendly with men in leadership in our church. Whether they were single or married, she flirted with all those she wanted attention from. She didn't have close female friends but attempted to make lots of male friends. She was very flirtatious.

One of the definitions of *seduction* is "someone inclined to mislead by flirtation, flattery, and whatever means of drawing attention to oneself."[4] Webster explains the word *flirt* to mean "someone who moves frequently from place to place, desiring to attract notice; to be pert (lively, *forward*; bold; saucy; *free to the point of not regarding established rules of respect of age, position, or station in life*); to be wanton (to go without restraint, rule, or limit; to live loosely); *apt to run off; lustful; lewd; having a playful sportive attitude without regularity or restraint* (being unpredictable at times)."[5] Maybe you've met someone like this.

Some girls are as bouncy and in your face as Tigger on Winnie the Pooh, showing up wherever the guys are, in order to get some attention, and wearing whatever they can find that looks sexy enough to attract them.

There is a difference in flirting and being friendly. Being friendly will cause a person to reach out to all people—both male and female. A friendly person is someone who is considerate of others' feelings, making them feel accepted and a part of the group. Their motives are pure when they meet people. They also understand boundaries in how they relate to the opposite sex, and they make a conscious effort not to appear forward in their friendliness toward the opposite sex. If they feel they are being taken wrongly by someone of the opposite sex, this type of woman will draw away completely from that guy so she doesn't feed any fuel to his fire. He will get the picture too. Friendliness from a pure motive is totally different from flirtation.

The flirtatious woman I mentioned finally latched on to a single Christian man who had been divorced and who previously had a lust problem. Although we advised them not to marry at the time, they found a justice of the peace to marry them one weekend. Within two months, they were divorced. Why did this happen? Even though they said they were Christians, the basis of their marriage was seduction and lust.

Not only was this woman seductive and flirtatious, she was also deceptive. Many of us felt great caution when around her. After the divorce, we received a letter from the husband saying how sorry he was for not listening to our advice to wait. He shared in the letter that he actually felt she had been involved in witchcraft as well.

The Snare of a Loose Woman

Queen Jezebel, the wife of Ahab, the king of Israel, was not only seductive and deceptive, but also controlling (see 1 Kings chapters 16–22). She served Baal (a god of satan). Ahab was easily seduced and controlled by her because he lived by lust and never surrendered to God. Where lust is not denied and crucified, seduction and demonic control will overtake a person.

The writer of Proverbs wrote to his son to keep God's commandments and His laws and allow them to reprove and instruct him. He said that the young man who lives by the Word of God will be kept from the loose woman who flatters with her words and seeks to capture a man with her eyes (see Prov. 6:20-26). This woman moves around to ensnare a man in order to bring him down.

Proverbs 5:20 says, *"Why should you, my son, be infatuated with a loose woman, embrace the bosom of an outsider, and go astray?"* (AMP). Proverbs 7:8-27 speaks of the seductive woman being a loose woman who uses smooth words. She watches and plans to entice and persuade a man to let go of his conscience and his fears in order to yield to and follow her solicitation, not showing him the path leading to death and hell ahead. Proverbs 30:20 says that she wipes her mouth after fulfilling her lust and says, *"I have done no wickedness"* (AMP). She dismisses any conviction in her heart of her wrongdoing and reasons away her actions by blaming others. There is no humility; she does not admit sin or repent of it.

Isaiah 3:16 speaks of women with an attitude of pride in their physical beauty and form, walking with necks stretched forth and wanton eyes (the Hebrew word for "wanton" as used here is *saqar* meaning deceiving and lying eyes). The Amplified says, *"Undisciplined (flirtatious and alluring) eyes, tripping along with mincing* [or small steps] *and affected gait, and making a tinkling noise with [the anklets on] their feet."*

Dake's Bible says that these women looked among the men to see whom they could capture by alluring, with a look of their eyes that was wanton (and lustful). Moffatt's and Berkley Bible Versions say that these women had "ogling eyes," meaning they looked at men with improper admiration and coarse familiarity. Familiarity breaks down boundaries of restraint. Sometimes Christians who fellowship or work together can become so relaxed they become vulnerable to emotional pulls from the opposite sex who are among them. Some Christian women who have not had healthy relationships can begin to have an improper admiration toward a male leader and then go beyond boundaries, pursuing that leader in an appropriate and wrong way.

I received a long-distance phone call once from a worship leader's wife. She shared how her husband led a worship team at church whom he spent a lot of time with. One young single woman on the team wore tight-fitting clothes and at times wore really short dresses with slits to reveal her legs. It didn't help any that she enjoyed joking around a lot with this woman's husband.

The worship team began to receive invitations to minister in other places, and the husband said there wasn't enough room to take his wife along, so she remained at home. The improper admiration and coarse familiarity of the young single woman toward the married worship leader had become a seduction. The man did not want to admit it, but his lust and pride had opened a door that should never have been opened. Then the worship leader began to talk to his wife about his dissatisfaction with their marriage relationship.

(Be cautious and watch out for familiarity and improper admiration from the opposite sex that allows a person to go beyond boundaries they should not exceed.) When someone gives in to seduction, it can take away everything he or she has gained.

Proverbs 7:21-27 says:

So she seduced him with her pretty speech, her coaxing and her wheedling [entices with soft words or flattery], *until he yielded to her. He couldn't resist her flattery. He followed her as an ox going to the butcher, or as a stag that is trapped, waiting to be killed with an arrow through its heart. He was as a bird flying into a snare, not knowing the fate awaiting it there. Listen to me, young men, and not only listen but obey; don't let your desires get out of hand; don't let yourself think about her. Don't go near her; stay away from where she walks, lest she tempt you and seduce you. For she has been the ruin of multitudes—a vast host of men have been her victims. If you want to find the road to hell, look for her house* (TLB).

"Wanton" is the opposite of "moral chastity." In First Timothy 2:9 the word "sobriety" or "soberminded" is the Greek word *sophrosune,* meaning moral chastity and self-control or discretion. Godly women were to be known by "moral chastity" and self-restraint.

Girls and women who are seeking to be godly understand there are boundaries that they must keep in as they relate to the opposite sex. Those who are seductive go beyond boundaries and push compromise in those they are trying to seduce. *A seducing spirit always wants attention!*

Seduction Can Mean Long-Term Heartache

Years ago I remember hearing the story of a handsome young Christian man who had experienced a call of God on his life as a teenager. Upon arriving at a Christian university to pursue this calling to the ministry, he met a beautiful young woman who professed to be a Christian and who was very attracted to him.

As she pursued him, he became distracted from his calling and deeply involved with the girl. She wanted more than a friendship relationship and wore clothes that pulled on his sexual desires. Consequently, the relationship moved into sexual involvement. His spirit immediately felt grieved over his actions, and he repented and pulled away from the relationship. However, her seduction had developed a strong grip on him. Although he tried to overcome, she wore down his resistance over a period of time. Finally, he decided to marry her because of the condemnation he felt regarding his sexual involvement with her.

Once married, he thought he could pursue his ministry calling, but she did not have the same desire for ministry. They had a child, but she was not happy. Eventually, she left him and the child for another man. Take note: A seducing spirit will never be satisfied. It may get what it wants and hide itself temporarily, but it will rise and attempt to lure again.

If a person does not realize that she is under the influence of a seducing spirit, that spirit will continue to work in her life and grow. It will also grow in its deceptiveness as well, covering up sin in order to keep practicing it (see Isa. 29:15; 30:1-3). The only way to cast off a controlling, seducing spirit is to first realize that you might be under its influence.

There are Christians in churches and Christian schools right now who are living under the influence and manipulation of a seducing spirit. In order to remove this spirit, it must be dealt with spiritually. It will not just go away.

Once a person realizes he or she is being controlled by seduction, the person must repent of it, bring her will into submission to God's will, and deny its power to ever control her again. Once this is done, the person must become and remain accountable to someone else who will help guide her in the right direction spiritually. Total honesty and a willingness to be examined in actions, thoughts, and choices are absolutely crucial in this kind of relationship. It requires a conscious effort to live godly. Seduction is very deceptive and strong in its control. A person has to keep an honest and open heart with someone else who loves her enough to confront her when needed.

After the young man's wife left him, he thought himself a failure and felt condemned, thinking he could never fulfill the call of God on his life. At this time of godly sorrow, the Lord spoke to him, revealing that He was raising him up again to minister healing and salvation to other people. He became a part of a ministry staff, and he ministered for several years as a single parent until one day God brought a godly young single woman into his life who was also fulfilling her call in ministry. Over the years, God has used them to minister to many people. God's mercy intervened in a life and saved many more lives afterwards.

A Word to Christian Women

Have you ever stopped to think about how you dress? How about the way you use your eyes? Do you use your body when you walk to attract attention? If you have examined yourself and you believe the motive of your heart is pure in the way you dress, in how you relate with guys, and in the way you talk, then you are not being wrongly influenced.

A godly person thinks about how she comes across to people. She uses discretion (the ability to avoid words, actions, and thoughts that could lead to undesirable consequences). She knows what is appropriate and what is not appropriate. She understands boundaries and she places boundaries on her life in the way she dresses and lives.

I remember trying to help a woman understand seduction. There were areas in her life that she needed to examine. I mentioned the name of a beautiful young single woman in our church who dressed modestly but with style. She had a testimony of purity. She chose not to date a lot, yet she was one of the most popular girls among the guys and girls at the university she attended. A girl doesn't have to seduce guys to be popular.

God needs girls and women in these times to stand up against the force of seduction and be a light to others. If we'll guard our hearts, we'll walk with pure motives and relate with the opposite sex in an appropriate and godly way. We will also attract healthy relationships.

Thoughts to Remember

Here are some closing thoughts to remember:

1. *Seduce* means "to draw aside or entice from the path of moral rectitude (or moral conduct of what is right) and duty (moral obedience and submission to God)."

2. Flattery esteems and praises a person for personal benefit, while a compliment has no ulterior motive except to esteem and encourage someone.

3. Reading and practicing the Word of God in your life and loving purity will help keep you from seduction.

4. Appointing a person to hold you accountable—a person you are totally open and honest with—will protect you from being seduced.

5. Seduction is a demonic spirit (see 1 Tim. 4:1). It is one of the signs of the last days. The more you continue to read God's Word and pray and are held accountable, the stronger your spirit will become to overcome the influence of seducing spirits.

6. If a young girl learns the power of her sexual persuasion early enough and how it can be used to help her get her way, she can become controlled by a seducing spirit for years. It becomes a lifestyle and a way of manipulating others. A seducing spirit always wants attention.

7. If your motives are pure, you will relate to the opposite sex in an appropriate and godly way.

Endnotes

1. Noah Webster, *1828 American Dictionary of the English Language*.

2. Ibid.

3. Ibid.

4. Ibid.

5. Ibid.

Chapter Thirteen

The "God Loves Me No Matter What" Mind-set

S OME Christians' view of their relationship with Jesus is, "God loves me no matter what. No matter what I do or don't do, He still loves me. Whether I obey Him or not, whether I live for Him or not, He loves me; and in either case, I will still go to Heaven someday."

This attitude allows a person to grant himself a license to sin. It implies there is no penalty or judgment for sin as long as someone believes in Jesus and accepts Him in a prayer at sometime in his or her life. If that is true, then people never need to repent when they get saved. There is no need to turn from a life of sin. However, God's Word says that repentance is a necessary part of salvation; you cannot have salvation without it (see Matt. 9:13; Mark 1:15; 6:12; Luke 13:3; Acts 2:38; 3:19). In fact, repentance is a gift God gives to us because He knows that in our humanness we will fail and need a way of escape.

John the Baptist, Jesus, and all the writers of the New Testament preached repentance. Paul actually described how to repent (see 2 Cor. 7:9-11). He explained it to an entire church that had already received Jesus Christ but struggled with sin.

Second Corinthians 5:10 indicates that we all will appear one day before the judgment seat of Christ and receive the things done in our bodies here on earth, whether good or bad. If we do not repent on earth, we will be judged for the bad. Yes, God loves us and will always love us. In fact, He loves us so much that He allows us to choose our own way, and He will not stop us. We've been given a free will. He wants us to choose to love Him, but He won't force us to love Him.

Turning Glory Into Shame

God has loved many people only to watch them go into hell for all eternity. Some have chosen to love God at one time, but when peer pressure, distractions, and seductive temptations came along, they gave up their love for God and chose to love the world system around them instead.

Second Peter 2:20-22 says:

For if after they have escaped the pollutions of the world through the knowledge of the Lord and Savior Jesus Christ, they are again entangled therein, and overcome, the latter end is worse with them than the beginning. For it had been better for them not to have known the way of righteousness, than, after they have known it, to turn from the holy commandment delivered unto them. But it is happened unto them according to the true proverb, The dog is turned to his own vomit again; and the sow that was washed to her wallowing in the mire.

Hebrews 10:39 says, "*But we are not of them who draw back unto perdition; but of them that believe to the saving of the soul.*" The word "perdition" is the Greek word *apoleia*, which means "destruction or damnation."[1]

Philippians 3:18-19 states:

*For many walk, of whom I have told you often, and now tell you even weeping, that they are the enemies of the cross of Christ: whose end is destruction, whose God is their belly, and whose glory is in their shame, **who mind earthly things*** (emphasis added).

Is your mind focused on enjoying the pleasures of this earth so much that you do not think about where you will spend eternity—Heaven or hell?

Both The Living Bible and The Amplified Bible say that the doom or fate of the unsaved and unrepentant is eternal misery because they live by their appetites and sensuality, and they actually are proud of what they should be ashamed of. The only life they think about is this life here on earth.

It's interesting that Paul says their *"glory is in their shame."* I was reading one day and came across a Scripture in Psalm 4:2 that made a strong impression upon my heart. *"O ye sons of men, how long will ye turn my glory into shame? how long will ye love **vanity**, and seek after **leasing**?"* (emphasis added).

Vanity means "emptiness and futility, fruitless desire; want of substance to satisfy desire; laboring for something that produces no good; thinking you're doing great (pride)."[2] *Futility* means "talking a lot but you have no weight and depth to you."[3] *Leasing*, as used in this verse, means "lying and falsehood (an old Anglo Saxon word)."[4] God is saying,

How long will you turn My glory that I've given to you into shame? How long will you chase after empty, fruitless desires that produce nothing good in your life, thinking you're doing fine? You are even able to talk to others with Christian words you've learned to say so that you can fit in with settings you need to fit into, but you have no spiritual depth. Instead, you are shallow. You choose to live a lie and you won't humble yourself to Me and admit your need, allowing Me to work in your life (author's paraphrase).

Selective Obedience

Some Christians have actually claimed that it doesn't matter how a Christian lives because "God looks on the heart." Let's take a look at the only place this phrase is used in Scripture.

In First Samuel chapter 8, we see that the people of Israel wanted a king like other nations had, instead of being ruled by God through His judges and prophets. God agreed to give them their request and had Samuel the prophet anoint Saul as king. (Note: It's interesting that even though people of God may ask for something out of a wrong motive, God will sometimes finally give them what they want. However, any desire that's influenced by wrong motivation will eventually bring trouble.)

Because Saul was taller than most other people, many Israelites admired his outward appearance. However, what they didn't *see was Saul's self-will. He obeyed God partially, just enough to look good.* This is called *selective obedience.* Many Christians today also select to obey just enough Scripture to look good and to prevent others from asking too many questions. In time, God became weary with Saul going his own way. Samuel repetitively warned Saul to obey God. (Warning: Christians who obey God partially or just enough to present a good front, while still living for themselves and the things of the world, will someday find that their hearts have become so hardened that they no longer are able to hear the voice of God.)

God made one final request of Saul. He was to destroy the Amalekites because of their hatred toward Israel. But instead of destroying all the Amalekites, Saul decided to keep Agag the king alive, along with the best of the sheep, oxen, lambs, and all that was good. We are not sure why Saul did not fully obey God's instructions. It could have been that Saul wanted to bring the king of the defeated nation back to parade before the people so they would admire and praise him for his victory, as was custom in Bible days. Saul was proud and insecure and needed people's admiration. Remember in First Samuel chapters 17 and 18, he became very jealous and threatened when he heard the people cheer young David for slaying Goliath. In any case, Saul wanted his position more than a relationship of hearing and obeying God.

When the prophet Samuel came to meet Saul, he had already been told by God what Saul had done. Saul came out to meet him and immediately said, "*May the Lord bless you! I have obeyed the Lord's commands*" (1 Sam. 15:13 NCV). Samuel then asked him why he could hear sheep and oxen making noise, catching Saul in his lie. Saul had to think fast to cover himself and responded that he had kept some of the animals to give as an offering and sacrifice to God. That sounded like a good "religious" reason, but that was not what God had told him to do.

Sometimes when a person wants to escape being caught in disobedience, he will lie. If lying doesn't work, he may then try to *reason why he did what he did and even use spiritual excuses*. When Samuel did not accept Saul's reason, Saul then blamed the people and declared that they made him do it. If lying doesn't work, then blame someone else. This is the pattern of someone who has learned to lie and live in selective obedience. Only when he runs out of lame excuses will he finally admit his sin. At this point he may cry, hoping that his emotions will play on the mercy of others who might let him off the hook and not hold him accountable. However, when a person realizes that he will not be held responsible and will not suffer any consequences, he will usually commit the sin again.

A Rebellious Heart

Samuel then told Saul that God wants obedience more than any sacrifice and because of his continual disobedience, the kingdom was being taken from him that day. God would give it to another person. Samuel went on to say, "*Rebellion is as the sin of witchcraft, and stubbornness is as iniquity and idolatry...*" (1 Sam. 15:23). The true sacrifice God wants from us is a broken and contrite spirit (see Ps. 51:17). This is not referring to someone who is broken down because of circumstances. It is referring to a heart that has become *humble and repentant* before God and obeys Him. *A person with a repentant heart is someone who is willing to admit sin immediately and turn away from anything that doesn't please God.* When a Christian has a humble heart, she will be easily convicted of sin in order to repent. She will also have a sensitivity to the Holy Spirit's voice and will have a desire to not go against what God has spoken.

God says rebellion is like witchcraft. Why? Witchcraft seeks to control. A rebellious person does what she wants instead of what God wants with her life. She wants to control her own life. God says that stubbornness to His will is sin and idolatry. Idolatry is putting anything before God. When we put our will before God's will, we make our will an idol. Our will must continually be brought into submission to God's will.

Have you ever resented a person in authority or a person who has told you not to do something that you really wanted to do? And you ask yourself, "Who do they think they are to tell me I can or can't do something that I want to do?" So stubbornly, you go ahead and do it. Your conscience deals with you, but you shove it aside, and you think that if you just don't get caught, you will be okay. And you may even get away with it. Let me assure you, the devil wants you to think that you're getting away with it—but it's only for a little while. You will be caught, and it will be hard.

God's Word reveals the characteristics of His will. Remember, *His will always honors Him.* And when we bring our will into submission to His will, we honor Him. The Scriptures say that if we choose our own way, we have despised God. "*I will honor only those who honor Me, and I will despise those who despise Me*" (1 Sam. 2:30 TLB).

After Samuel and Saul's conversation, Saul wanted the situation between him and Samuel to appear as if everything was just fine before the people. He asked the prophet to turn with him to the people like they were still great friends and go together to worship God. Samuel loved Saul and did as he requested, but the anointing as leader lifted at that moment from Saul; and he could no longer hear God's voice. He was on his own. From then on, he lived under Satan's oppression and died a tragic death.

The Lord Looks at the Heart

After the anointing for king was taken from Saul, the Lord told Samuel to go to the house of Jesse, the Bethlehemite where He had chosen one of Jesse's sons to reign over Israel. When Samuel arrived and Jesse brought all his sons into the house, Samuel became caught up with the oldest son's outward appearance and consequently thought he must be God's choice for king. He was tall and had a natural look of a leader. Since Eliab was the oldest, his father Jesse also probably looked to him to lead his younger brothers. He just seemed to be the obvious choice. But God said to Samuel, "*Do not look at his appearance or at the height of his stature, because I have rejected him; for God sees not as man sees, for man looks at the outward appearance, but **the Lord looks at the heart**" (1 Sam. 16:7 NASB, emphasis added). God looks for a heart who loves Him, who wants to obey Him, and who believes in Him. He knows those who seek to know Him and trust in Him. He looks for those who believe that they can do whatever He needs them to do.

All the sons passed before Samuel, but God rejected each one. Samuel then asked if there were any others, and Jesse called in his youngest son, David, who had been tending sheep. God told Samuel to anoint David in the midst of his brothers, and the Spirit of God came upon him. God wanted the older ones to see that His hand was upon David.

Some people have casually used the statement, "Oh, well, God looks on the heart," as a means to live any way they want and dress any way they want, reasoning that no matter what they do, God knows somewhere deep down in their heart they still love Him. On the contrary, *real love proves itself*. God did not accept Saul's casual *attitude of selective obedience*. The Bible says He rejected him, because Saul rejected God's Word (see 1 Sam. 15:26). Whereas, in Acts 13:22 God said, "*I have found David the son of Jesse, **a man after Mine own heart**, which shall fulfill all My will*" (emphasis added).

In First Samuel chapter 16, when God sent Samuel to Jesse's home to anoint one of Jesse's sons as the next king, God's choice wasn't any of the sons that Jesse and Samuel thought would be chosen. God was looking for the heart of a young man who was seeking Him, and that man happened to be young David. *God looks on the heart of everyone to see who will fulfill His will.*

David was a lover of God even as a shepherd boy when no one else was around but sheep. His love for God fueled his desire to please God and to obey Him.

Later, when David became king, he still proved his love for God and sought to obey God. The Bible does tell us, however, that years after becoming king, David did, at times, fail. On one occasion he did not go out to battle per God's will, but stayed home. In doing so, he put himself in a vulnerable situation and fell for a trap that satan had set up. He committed adultery with a woman and then had her husband killed.

David committed sin just as Saul had; however, there was one very important difference. David knew he had sinned and when he was confronted, he was ashamed and grieved over his sin. More than anything, it seemed that he grieved about breaking his communion relationship with God. His relationship with God meant more to him than his position as king. Over and over he spoke of how God's presence in his life meant everything to him. At this time of recognition and confession of sin, he wrote the words of Psalm 51. In this chapter, he poured out his soul in repentance and asked God not to remove His Spirit from him. He cried out to God that out of this experience, he would teach transgressors His ways. This awakening brought great brokenness and change in his life.

When we truly understand that God looks on the heart, we must realize the seriousness of submitting our lives to Him, obeying Him, and loving Him more than this world and all that it offers. If we sin, it should grieve our hearts and stir us to repentance and greater awareness of our humanness and the spiritual battle we face. It should motivate us to honor God all the more.

Love For This World or Love For God

A sad situation is revealed in Second Timothy 4:10 when Paul writes about Demas, *a fellow Christian minister*. Paul says, *"Demas hath forsaken me, **having loved this present world**..."* (emphasis added). There are Christians and even some in ministry today who love this world and its ways more than total obedience to God. Are we conforming to this world more than conforming to Christ? Have we related to this world to such an extent that we have become like the world? James 4:4 says,

"Know ye not that the friendship of the world [its way of thinking] *is enmity with God?"*

First John 2:15-17 says:

Stop loving this evil world and all that it offers you, for when you love these things you show that you do not really love God; for all these worldly things, these evil desires—the craze for sex, the ambition to buy everything that appeals to you, and the pride that comes from wealth and importance—these are not from God. They are from this evil world itself. And this world is fading away, and these evil, forbidden things will go with it, but whoever keeps doing the will of God will live forever (TLB).

Notice, John wrote, *"Whoever keeps doing the will of God will live forever."* Then in First John 5:3 he writes, *"Loving God means doing what He tells us to do..."* (TLB). If you say, "I love Jesus," but your life reflects that you are living your own will, showing no outward desire to do God's will, you're actually lying. God is the One who says so in First John 1:6.

We need to check our hearts regularly. Second Corinthians 13:5 says, *"Examine yourselves, whether ye be in the faith; prove your own selves. Know ye not your own selves, how that Jesus Christ is in you, except ye be reprobates?"*

Reprobate is the "condition of a person who is abandoned to sin; lost to virtue; does not have a standard of purity; abandoned to error or in apostasy."[5]

Paul wrote to Titus that there were some who *"profess that they know God; but in works they deny Him, being abominable, and disobedient, and unto every good work reprobate"* (Titus 1:16). Why would Paul have spent time writing letters to churches regarding living a holy, consecrated life if it was simply okay to do whatever you want to do because "God looks on the heart"?

Following God or Following the Crowd

If we don't seek to know God and want God, we will become conformed to this world around us and become vulnerable to its deception. The time you take regularly with God in learning His Word and in talking to Him will deliver you in the days ahead.

God's Word is our standard of measure. We must hold our lives to His measuring rod and judge ourselves whether or not we are walking in line with its counsel. When some Christians measure themselves with the friends they hang around with, they come to the conclusion that they're doing pretty good or at least as good as so-and-so. Second Corinthians 10:12 says that when Christians measure themselves with each other and their own little ideas, it is stupidity (TLB). You might be following the kind of friends like a herd of cows follows other cows who are to be slaughtered!

In Exodus chapter 32, Moses and Joshua had been away from the camp of the Israelites in order to seek God and receive His commands. As the two men came down the mountain, they could hear a lot of noise below among the people. Joshua thought maybe the people were being stirred to go to war, but Moses knew in his spirit that it wasn't a sound of warfare but a sound of celebration.

When they reached the people, they found them drinking, dancing, and partying around a golden calf they had made and placed in the middle of the camp. Moses took the commandments in stone that God had supernaturally written for the people to live by, and he broke them, signifying that they had broken God's command of loving Him more than anything or anyone else. Their desire to party and live for themselves was more than their love for God. Aaron, who had been left in charge as their spiritual leader, had simply given the people what they wanted.

Even today, some Christian leaders will sacrifice pleasing God in order to please people because they want to remain in charge of those people. (Actually, the people are in control of the leader.) Moses had to stand before the people and be bold enough to call them to make a decision, whether or not they would follow after God. The ones who chose not to follow after God were destroyed.

If the Christian crowd you're hanging out with isn't following after God, it is wise to change directions and go with those who are. Don't end up losing what you've received from God (see Heb. 2:1-3).

So, how does this subject relate to modesty? Modesty is based upon a surrendered heart that wants to please God. Sometimes you may have to go against the crowd in order to follow God and do what He says. When it comes to the way we dress and what we do, we have to decide who we want to please—God or the crowd.

Thoughts to Remember

Here are some closing thoughts to remember:

1. God will always love you, but each of us will one day stand before the judgment seat of Christ and receive in accordance with what we have done in the earth, whether good or bad. If we haven't repented of the bad while living on earth, we will be judged for it. Repentance is a gift.

2. Repentance is being willing to admit sin and turn away from it. A repentant person is easily convicted of sin and sensitive to the voice of the Holy Spirit. She does not want to go against what God has spoken.

3. Because love is a choice, God will let you choose to go your own way or go His way. You've been given a free will. God wants you to love Him by a choice of your own will.

4. Selective obedience means you obey just enough Scripture to look good. Your partial obedience provides an outward cover to make people think you are completely obedient. God wants total obedience and not partial obedience with some sacrifices of praise thrown in. Rebellion is as witchcraft, and stubbornness is as sin and idolatry. Just as witchcraft wants control, rebellion wants control. Just as an idol becomes something a person worships, some people worship their own stubborn will. They stubbornly do what they want instead of worshiping God and doing His will.

5. God looks on the heart of everyone to see if the heart is going after Him and if that heart will fulfill everything He commands. God found David to be a man after His heart. God knows the heart who is following Him and the heart who isn't.

6. Loving God means doing what He tells you to do. When someone says, "I love Jesus," but her life reflects that she wants to do her own will and she shows no outward desire to do God's will, she is actually lying (see 1 John 1:6; 5:3).

7. Sometimes you have to be different than the crowd when they are going their own direction and not

God's direction. You have to decide in your heart who you want to please.

Endnotes

1. Dake, NT, 218.

2. Noah Webster, *1828 American Dictionary of the English Language*.

3. Ibid.

4. Ibid.

5. Ibid.

Chapter Fourteen

So What's the Big Deal About Surrender?

EVERYTHING about being a Christian, from start to finish, is based upon *surrender*. *Surrender* is the "act of yielding or resigning your life or the possession of something into the power of another; to give up or yield to the influence, passion, or power of another."[1] Surrender is based on love. When you truly love someone, you surrender your own plans based on your independent life, and instead you do that which considers the other person. You think about how your actions affect another person.

In surrender to Jesus, you now think about how your actions affect your relationship with Him and with others. You will find that your surrender to Jesus is not just a one-time experience you have had at sometime in your past. It becomes a daily experience. You choose to surrender to His will every day instead of going your own way or demanding your own way. Those who understand the *surrendered heart* know that when you go your own way or choose to be strong willed or self-focused, you'll run into that inner convicting voice of the Holy Spirit (and your conscience) telling you to stop and change. I know this for a fact, because I have run into that still small voice of the Holy Spirit many times.

When you surrender to Jesus, you recognize that you no longer belong to yourself. You belong to God. *He owns* you now that you've invited Jesus into your heart as Lord and Savior. By the way, He can't just be Savior without becoming Lord. He comes in as both Savior and Lord, and He comes in as the new owner of your house and is your personal interior and exterior decorator.

Your New Owner

Once you become a Christian, you need to recognize that your body and your spirit are now God's dwelling place or house. He is your new owner.

> *Haven't you yet learned that your body is the home of the Holy Spirit God gave you, and that He lives within you?* **Your own body does not belong to you.** *For God has bought you with a* **great price.** *So* **use every part of your body to give glory back to God, because He owns it** (1 Corinthians 6:19-20 TLB, emphasis added).

Believe me, *God cares about His house.* Think about it. If you own a house, you don't want someone else deciding how that house will be painted, decorated, furnished, and maintained. The owner makes all these types of decisions within and without. Some Christians want Jesus to be with them to help them out when they get into trouble (like a maintenance man), but they don't want Him telling them how to decorate their house or what they can do and cannot do in maintaining their house.

Some Christians only want a ticket to Heaven (just a Savior). They don't really want Jesus to have ownership (or lordship), because they want to own themselves. A self-ownership mentality says, "I'm free. I can do what I want to do. No one can tell me what I have to do or what I have to wear."

But remember, Jesus paid the highest price for you (and your house). He paid in blood—the blood of His Father God (see 1 Pet. 1:18-21), and that blood supernaturally cleanses your sin. Jesus' blood has the power to keep you healed, delivered, and protected from the thief or the robber who would like to break in and steal what's in your house. But Jesus can only protect the house if He has *full ownership rights to your house and He's the only One with the key*.

You need to make sure the doors and windows to your house are closed and locked. Any homeowner knows that you never give the key to some smooth-talking guy who comes along to check out your property. When you have your personal time with God each day, acknowledge that you know He owns you and you want Him to keep you and lead you so that your house won't be robbed or broken into.

Your Choices Are Critical

Did you know that your life—whether or not it is a good life or a difficult life—is determined by choices you make daily, living submitted and surrendered to God or living your own way. The choices and decisions you make will affect your future. Jesus understood the power of choice, and He chose to live submitted and surrendered even in the face of great temptation. He showed us that it is possible for humans to submit their will and surrender to God. God gave humans free will because He wanted us to love Him and obey Him by our own choice. God won't force us, even though He knows the end result of an unsubmitted will is heartache, pain, hardship, and sometimes destruction.

So when Christians know that the Bible says to live a surrendered life, why do they ignore that knowledge? They want to fulfill their own desires or lust.

When you decide to go your own way, it's as if you unlock and open doors or windows to the invader (satan). Sometimes Christians wonder why their lives are full of heartache and difficulty, but if they would take time to reevaluate the choices they've made, they would probably discover incidences that caused them to become more vulnerable. At these times, they stubbornly insist on going their own direction instead of obeying God's promptings and warnings. When you are self-willed, stubborn, rebellious, and unsubmissive to God's authority, the enemy has much greater opportunity to rob from you and could even destroy you.

Considering Jesus

Surrender means considering Jesus about everything. Hebrews 12:3 says, "*Consider Him* [Jesus]...." *Consider* means "to think seriously; to have regard for; to respect; to take into view in examination."[2] When you consider Jesus, you think about His opinion and His view of things. You want your attitudes, thoughts, motives, words, behavior, and yes, even your dress and appearance to *honor* Him. You think about pleasing Him more than pleasing yourself or anyone else. Ask yourself, "Do I consider Jesus in what I wear, what I think, what I say, and what I do?" You also think about how you are representing Jesus to others.

Are people attracted to Jesus when they look at you, or are they simply attracted to your body? Ask yourself as a Christian, "Do I look any different than those in the world around me?" A friend of mine said that when she gets up to dress each morning before leaving for work, she looks in the mirror and asks herself, "Would Jesus be comfortable with what I am wearing?" or "Would what I am wearing embarrass or disappoint Him?

Serious Christians are willing to conduct self-evaluation checks. Real Christians don't mind asking themselves, "Can people see Jesus in the way I live? Does my lifestyle—the way I dress as well as the words I speak—help or hinder people in becoming closer to Jesus? Romans 14:7 says, *"For none of us liveth to himself, and no man dieth to himself."* This verse in The Living Bible says, *"We are not our own bosses...."* Romans 14:13 says, *"Try instead to live in such a way that you will never make your brother stumble by letting him see you doing something he thinks is wrong"* (TLB).

T.L. Osborn, an international evangelist who has reached thousands of people around the world, said, "You are painting a picture of Jesus to others by every word you speak and every deed you do. Make sure you are painting a good picture."

Once you decide to surrender your life to Jesus, you won't have difficulty obeying God's Word. You will begin to see it as a guideline to help you live.

Thoughts to Remember

Here are some closing thoughts to remember:

1. Once you have surrendered your life to Jesus, you will think about how your actions affect your relationship with Him and with others. Surrender is not a one-time experience. Surrender to God is daily—daily surrendering your attitudes, your thoughts, and your choices to Him.

2. Surrender to Jesus means that when you are born again, you now surrender your body and spirit to God and you are now His dwelling place (His house). He owns you and has a right to direct how you decorate the house.

3. Your quality of life will be determined by the daily choices you make.

4. God calls us to live in such a way that we will not cause another person to stumble in their walk with the Lord (see Rom. 14:13 TLB).

5. International evangelist, T.L. Osborn, said, "You are painting a picture of Jesus to others by every word you speak and every deed you do." Are you painting a good picture? Are people attracted to Jesus when they look at you, or are they simply attracted to your body?

Endnotes

1. Noah Webster, *1828 American Dictionary of the English Language.*

2. Ibid.

Chapter Fifteen

The Process of Being Changed

WHEN you become a Christian, you aren't immediately aware of or have a full knowledge of all the guidelines and instructions for life. It's a learning process. But if you are truly surrendered to God, you want to learn and do what He says. God understands the stages of our growth process, and He works with us to change us more and more into the image of His Son, Jesus (see 2 Cor. 3:18.) He knows you are not perfect. He understands your humanness, and He will work with you as you grow spiritually.

Never give up on yourself because He doesn't give up on you. As long as you desire God and you want to do His will, He will help you. Even when you fail, He will help you change for the better if you wanted to be helped.

When you choose to live in surrender to God, you will be *changed*—not everything will change immediately, but it will happen over a process of time. God wants you to think like Him and act like Him here in the earth. It's called becoming godly. The Bible uses another phrase—"being transformed."

Being Transformed and Renewing Your Mind

I appeal to you therefore, brethren, and beg of you in view of [all] the mercies of God, to make a decisive dedication of your bodies [presenting all your members and faculties] as a living sacrifice, holy (devoted, consecrated) and well pleasing to God, which is your reasonable (rational, intelligent) service and spiritual worship. Do not be conformed to this world (this age), [fashioned after and adapted to its external, superficial customs], but be transformed (changed) by the [entire] renewal of your mind [by its new ideals and its new attitude], so that you may prove [for yourselves] what is the good and acceptable and perfect will of God, even the thing which is good and acceptable and perfect [in His sight for you] (Romans 12:1-2 AMP).

Transformed means "to change the form, to change the appearance; to be renewed; metamorphosis—like a caterpillar changing into a butterfly."[1] In fact, the Greek word for "transformed" is *metamorphoo*, a supernatural change by renewing of the mind. Many Christians are saved but never go on to renew their minds to the Word of God. You renew your mind by reading, studying, memorizing, and praying God's Word daily. As I stated earlier, it's not legalism; it's a spiritually healthy habit. We benefit from renewing our minds to the Word of God, and others appreciate the fact that we are not as difficult to live with or be around.

When we desire to read and apply God's Word to our lives, it affects how we live and relate with other people. We become better people than we were before because we start adjusting our lives to His Word.

Romans 12:1-2 reads:

Therefore, I urge you, brothers, in view of God's mercy, to offer your bodies as living sacrifices, holy and pleasing to God—this is your spiritual act of worship. Do not conform [The Amplified says, "Do not be fashioned after"] any longer to the pattern [The Living Bible says "behavior and customs"] of this world, but be transformed by the renewing of your mind. Then you will be able to test and approve what God's will is—His good, pleasing and perfect will (NIV).

The Greek here is, "Do not conform or pattern your ways of living after this age or the times you are living in."

Verse 2 says the way you are transformed is by renewing your mind with the Word of God. You renew your thinking and it changes your behavior.

Romans 12:1 says, "[I] *beg of you...to make a decisive dedication of your bodies* [and your thinking]...*to God, which is your reasonable (rational, intelligent) service and spiritual worship*" (AMP). Consecrate yourself to Him. Live to please Him. This verse says that living to please God is part of our worship of God. This verse tells us that worship is not just singing songs, but is also how we live our lives. When we live to please God, we are worshiping God. When we live to please ourselves or the lust of others, you could say that we are worshiping our desires or others' desires instead of God. Wow! Those are pretty strong words. God wants first place. He owns you now, and He's jealous for you (see Ex. 34:14) because He loves you. He wants to rule you. This is the most excellent way because when He rules, He delivers us from all heartache and trouble.

Listening to His Voice

It's up to you to make a decisive dedication of yourself to God every day. Then, stay sensitive to His voice and obey Him. His voice talks to us two ways and it's our responsibility to listen:

1. He speaks to us in *His written Word.* We need to read the Bible daily in order to know what He likes and doesn't like, what will help us and what won't help us. The Word of God is our instruction manual to live by so we can keep ourselves from unnecessary heartache, pain, or destruction.

2. He speaks to us by *His Holy Spirit* who is now inside our hearts. He sends us promptings and thoughts of direction.

Second Corinthians 3:17-18 says:

Now the Lord is the Spirit [in other words, the Lord and the Holy Spirit are the same], *and where the Spirit of the Lord is, there is freedom* [The original Greek meaning here is, "Where the Spirit of the Lord is allowed to be Lord, there is freedom." We know that the Spirit of the Lord is omnipresent (everywhere), but people are not free everywhere. True freedom comes where He is allowed to be Lord and ruler of our choices and directions we take]. *And we, who with unveiled faces all reflect the Lord's glory, are being transformed* [changed] *into His likeness with ever-increasing glory, which comes from the Lord, who is the Spirit* (NIV).

When we listen and obey the thoughts of direction that the Holy Spirit speaks to us, we will continue to be *changed* into His likeness. *In other words, people will not wonder whether or not you are a Christian.* They will see it by the way you live. Webster's Dictionary says transformation changes one's whole appearance. Romans 12:1-2 and Second Corinthians 3:17-18 indicate that we will be changed in our whole lives while we are here on earth, more and more into His likeness, when we allow His Spirit and His Word to work in us. But there's a definite battle raging—the world wants our lives to move in a direction other than God's.

The J.B. Phillips Version of Romans 12:2 says, *"Don't let the world around you squeeze you into its own mold...."* This world definitely is trying to mold everyone. This world, the media—TV, movie, music videos, Internet, magazines—wants to mold your thinking. In fact, one music video star who appeared on MTV said that its mission is to change the way people in the world think and they know they have power to do it through the media. Let's face it, people watch TV, read magazines, and want to look like who they watch. But God says, "Don't let the world around you squeeze you into its own mold...."You have to make a decision to reject the voice of the world.

We all have a desire to stay in touch with fashion, but as Christians, we have to choose the fashions that stay within the boundaries of our first love, Jesus. Fashion designers change fashion yearly with most of society following their changes. And it's obvious that they are not fashioning clothes by the measuring stick of God's holy standards. Instead, they are led by the ungodly spirit of this world system, which lives by no restraints. We, as Christians, can stand and still dress in fashion, yet within boundaries of what is godly.

Ephesians 2:2 states, *"You went along with the crowd and were just like all the others, full of sin, obeying satan, the mighty prince of the power of the air, who is at work right now in the hearts of those who are against the Lord"* (TLB). Many times Christians don't realize that when they choose the fashionable way of the world around them, they are being led by another spirit other than the Spirit of God. They become a *mixture*—a little of God and a little of the world, not realizing they are gradually drifting away from the voice of God and the absolutes in His Word.

You Are Valuable

It boils down to understanding our value isn't in our clothes or physical bodies. It's not about our beauty. It isn't in our talents or even our personalities. It's not about how smart we are or what school we go to. It's not about how much money we make or the nice car or house we possess. Our value is not even about the family we live with, neither is it about the friends we make. *Our value is about the One who created us and loves us.*

You are valuable first of all because God created you and God doesn't create any junk. He chose for you to live on earth right now at this hour. You are made in the image of God. Animals, birds, and fish were not created like you. They were created after their kind (see Gen. 1:21-25). You were created out of God's kind after His likeness and in His image. God made you to be a reflection of Himself (see Gen. 1:26-31, 2:7,18-23). (You did not evolve from monkeys. If that were so, why have monkeys stopped evolving into people?) God created you uniquely special. You are different than any other person. Just like every snowflake is different, every human is different. He created you for His glory (see Ps. 8:3-9). You were created special as a human to fulfill God's purpose here on earth.

In Genesis chapter 3, we read that man and woman sinned, causing disorder in the earth. Because of sin and disorder, there have been many painful difficulties and consequences that mankind has suffered for centuries. In spite of this, God still considers every person born as valuable. You are uniquely made by God for His purposes and He loves you.

The psalmist wrote:

[Lord], *You made all the delicate, inner parts of my body, and knit them together in my mother's womb. Thank You for making me so wonderfully complex! It is amazing to think about...* (Psalm 139:13-14 TLB).

Verses 15-16 in the King James Version read:

My substance was not hid from thee, when I was made in secret....Thine eyes did see my substance, yet being unperfect; and in Thy book all my members were written, which in continuance were fashioned, when as yet there was none of them.

Verses 17-18 state:

How precious it is, Lord, to realize that You are thinking about me constantly! I can't even count how many times a day Your thoughts turn towards me. And when I waken in the morning, You are still thinking of me! (TLB).

Jeremiah wrote that God said, "*Before I formed thee in the belly I knew thee; and before thou camest forth out of the womb I sanctified* [separated] *thee, and I ordained thee a prophet unto the nations*" (Jer. 1:5). God knows each person before he is even formed in a woman's womb. You see, you and I come from the Father God Himself. When we realize this and accept Him as our Father and receive Jesus as Lord, we can fulfill our purpose of being here on earth. We are valuable because we were created by Him. God thought about you before the foundations of the world were ever made. You were in His plan to one day be on earth (see Eph. 2:10; Rev. 4:11).

Sometimes people think that because they were born "out of wedlock" or born in the midst of drugs, witchcraft, alcohol, or immorality, they aren't as valuable as someone else. *The conditions you were born in do not constitute your value.* You originated from God. The fact that others have sinned against God and you came in the midst of it does not change God's value of you or His desire and plan for your life.

In Jeremiah 29:11, God says that His plans for your life are for good and not for evil, to give you a future and a hope. However, realize that there is a thief (the devil) who comes to steal from your life, who will try to kill and destroy your life. Jesus lets us know that He came to give us life and give us life that is better than what we've known (see John 10:10).

You are also valuable because Jesus loves you and laid down His life for you. Think about it. Jesus died for you so you could live. No man will ever love you more than Jesus Christ.

"But [you were purchased] with the precious blood of Christ..." (1 Pet. 1:19 AMP). *"You were bought with a price [purchased with a preciousness and paid for, made His own]. So then, honor God and bring glory to Him in your body"* (1 Cor. 6:20 AMP).

The value of any item is measured by the price paid for it. The highest price possible was paid for you. No amount of money measures up to the blood of Jesus and the agony, pain, and horror He went through for you. He thinks you are worth a lot. Don't listen to thoughts that say you aren't worth much. You are valuable! Now rise up and begin to live like a valuable person.

Your Value Is Not in Your Body

It is important to understand that your value isn't in your body. You don't have to have the perfect body, but neither should you become lackadaisical about your looks. In addition, you don't have to show a lot of your body in order to get attention and feel valuable. Some girls and women think that if they show more of their body, they will get attention and feel valuable. You'll definitely get attention when you show a lot of skin, but realize that this kind of attention will cause others to use you, abuse you, then drop you until one day you're worn out and question your value again.

I've talked to women who were at one time physically beautiful and thought that fulfillment in life would come by showing their bodies and having guys lust for them. Some went from one relationship to another, and finally came to God for healing and restoration. Some were dancers in bars; others were prostitutes. But when their bodies changed and got older or they had babies, their boyfriends wanted to move on to new territory and their bosses wanted "fresh meat." The heartache came, and their sense of value was shaken.

When we base value on how we look or how we perform, we'll be hurt, disappointed, bitter, or may even think of self-destruction. But when you realize that Jesus loves you, there is freedom. He frees you from trying to find your identity in yourself and trying to find it through men's admiration.

Insecure people are always struggling to gain admiration, attention, and acceptance from others. On the other hand, secure people are at peace that the relationship they have with Jesus will ultimately cause them to have acceptance and favor with others and healthy relationships.

Your identity now that you are a Christian is "in Christ." When you begin to search and learn to pray the Scriptures over your life of being "in Him," "of Him," and what you can do "through Him," it begins to form a new image in your mind of who you are. He gives you a sense of security and confidence to live for Him and not be intimidated by others.

Danielle Baca, one of the "Out of Eden" sisters who sings in the Christian rhythm and blues hip-hop group, says that young women are looking for security in the wrong places, and as a result, they are putting the emphasis on external beauty rather than on what is in their hearts. "We as Christian women want to feel beautiful—you know what I mean? We do our hair, we put on makeup, but we have to understand that we have Jesus as our security, and understand who we are in Christ." He then shows us our value is in Him and that is what matters. Consequently, we're able to relate to other people in the right way.

Jesus Can Restore You

Even if you've made mistakes in your past, you can be forgiven and restored. In Christ your life becomes new and He is then able to work His plans and purposes in and through you. Second Corinthians 5:17 says, "[Whatever was of your] *old [previous moral and spiritual condition] has passed away. Behold, the fresh and new has come!*" (AMP). Think about it! Now that you are identified with Him, it is in Him that you live and move and have your being (see Acts 17:28).

It is also freedom to know that your identity is no longer limited to your natural family. Even though you may love your natural family, your identity is not in your family as much as your identity is in *Jesus Christ*. He's the One you want to grow up and be like.

Jesus is now our role model. He is who we should admire and want to be like in the way we think, the way we act, and the way we talk. He is our best example and who we should pattern our lives after. He's the only One who has never messed up, and He loves us even in our humanness. He believes in you and that you can change.

Instead of being conformed to or squeezed into the way the world views things, you can begin to let God's Word change your thinking and views to fit His way of thinking. God knows that our lives can change only as our thinking changes to His way of thinking. He said that as a person thinks in her heart, so is she (see Prov. 23:7).

Romans 13:14 says, *"But clothe yourself with the Lord Jesus Christ (the Messiah) and make no provision for [indulging] the flesh..."* (AMP). Dake's Translation says, "To take upon one, or to be clothed with, the interests of another; to enter into his views and be wholly (not partly) on his side, imitating him in all things], and don't give an opportunity for the flesh, to fulfil its lusts."² He not only tells us to study His Word to know His way of thinking, but He also instructs us to remove ourselves from any situation that would cause us temptation or would drag us down spiritually. He knows what feeds lust and what destroys it.

Jesus wants you to think the way He thinks. He thinks about everything that concerns you—even the clothes you wear. When you go shopping for clothes, consider or think about how He views what you are buying. Remember, He wants to protect you because you are valuable to Him. He knows how guys think and what triggers their imaginations. Believe me, if you are really listening to Jesus, He won't let you buy the tempting clothes. He'll make sure you are covered.

God's Fashion Statement Is Always "Holy"

Through the years, my husband and two sons would take notice if they thought that I or our two daughters needed some advice on what we were wearing. Sometimes our boys actually took the liberty to tell other girls (who were friends) if they felt what they were wearing was showing too much, and their friends appreciated it. Some girls don't have the benefit of receiving that kind of advice, but God will definitely talk to your heart about your clothes if you will listen.

The following is a testimony of a young single woman in our church who was saved in college and began to learn the Word of God and renew her mind. She wrote:

> I began serving the Lord wholeheartedly shortly after college graduation. As I matured in Him by reading His Word, being in church, attending home cell groups, and establishing godly friendships, I began to question some of my old habits like the music I listened to, the movies I watched, and the clothes I wore.

She shared that one day she heard the voice of the Holy Spirit say to "clean house." She went into her closet and looked at her clothes. They appeared okay—fashionable, good quality, and well maintained. However, she called her close friend and accountability partner and asked her if she felt that she dressed inappropriately or seductively. Her response shocked her. "Yes, 90 percent of the time." She couldn't believe her ears. Her immediate response was, "I have a curvy figure and I can't help it. Big clothes fall off me because I have a small waist." Another response was, "I'm single. Aren't we supposed to look cute? I can't walk around looking like a nun!" Her friend replied that she loved her but had to honestly say that she still dressed provocatively.

She then asked the Holy Spirit to help her. He began to show her some of her behavior patterns and how it was affecting other people. She continued:

> I was not taking into account that I had gotten bigger than the size "two" I was in college and that my clothes did not fit the same way they did before. Sometimes knowing my clothes were tight-fitting, I would wear them anyway, hoping that I looked the same way I did in them when I bought them years before. I was deceived. I was also a hindrance to some young men in the church who

on two occasions spoke to me about my inappropriate outfits which had caused guys difficulties with their thoughts toward me.

After discovering the truth and a few more spiritual closet cleanings later, she said God blessed her with new clothes that were more modest to conceal her figure, yet they were "hip" fashionably.

Both her male and female friends noticed her change and because she was a leader, some of the other girls began making changes too. *What you do always affects someone else.*

First Peter 1:14-15 says, *"As obedient children, not fashioning yourselves according to the former lusts in your ignorance* [God's fashion will always be "holy." There's no getting around it.]: *But as he which hath called you is holy, so be ye holy in all manner of conversation."* You can dress in fashion and still cover things that need to be covered.

Thoughts to Remember

Here are some closing thoughts to remember:

1. You are in process. God understands your humanness. He will change you as you allow Him. Transformation comes as you renew your mind to the Word of God.

2. Romans 12:1-2—Don't be conformed to this world's view, but instead let God transform your way of thinking to His way of thinking.

3. You are valuable because God created you and everything He creates is valuable. *He doesn't make any*

*junk.*You were created in His image after His likeness. You were uniquely created for His glory. You did not evolve from a monkey. You were created special as a human to fulfill God's purpose here on earth.

4. You are valuable, not because of your talents, abilities, money, educational training, perfect figure body, friends you hang out with, family lineage, good looks, beauty, or where you live; you are valuable because of the price that was paid to save you. Jesus gave His life for you. He wants to be in relationship with you. He loves you! *The value of an item is determined by the price paid for it. Jesus paid the highest price possible for you because He loves you!*

5. Your identity is now "in Christ." Those who do not become renewed in their mind to being in Christ are insecure. They struggle to gain admiration, attention, and acceptance from others. Secure people have a peace that their relationship with Jesus will bring them acceptance, and favor with others whenever they need it.

6. God's fashion statement is holy. (1 Pet. 1:14-15.) You can dress in fashion and still cover things that need to be covered.

Endnotes

1. Noah Webster, *1828 American Dictionary of the English Language.*
2. Dake, NT, 171.

Chapter Sixteen

The Love Test

IF we measure everything we do or say by the love test, we can determine whether or not we're being led by the Holy Spirit or by our own human lust. *Agape* love and lust are opposites. The primary focus of *agape* is God. It does what benefits others above benefiting itself. Lust, on the other hand, is self-focused. Lust does what will benefit itself even if it hurts or disappoints others. Lust simply wants to fulfill its desires.

Jesus tells us that the greatest commandment that we are to live our lives by is love. First, He says we are to love God more than anything in this world with all of our heart, soul, mind, and strength (see Mark 12:30). When you love God like this, you want to please Him, considering whether your actions or words are causing Him sorrow or joy. Loving God is not just mentally agreeing that we are to love Him. It's not just singing songs of love to Him at church. Love requires action and proof. John 14:21,24 says, "*The person who has My commands and keeps them is the one who [really] loves Me....Anyone who does not [really] love Me does not observe and obey My teaching...*" (AMP). When we really love God, we want to obey Him and live according to all He has already spoken to us in His Word. Some Christians want to select only the Scriptures they like and ignore or toss out the rest. But those who really love God are willing to be corrected by His Word and want to please Him more than anything.

Secondly, Jesus said we are to love others as much as we love ourselves (see Mark 12:31). People who love themselves care about themselves, but Jesus explains that we should want to also care about how we are affecting others around us. The golden rule says, "*Do unto others as you would have them do unto you.*" (Matt. 7:12) If you would not want some other woman dressing seductive to take your husband or your son into sexial sin, then don't you dress in a seductive way that would cause another woman's husband or son to sin.

Paul wrote that if we walk in this kind of love, we will obey all of God's laws. We won't want to harm, seduce, or cheat, deceive, kill, or steal from others. We will keep ourselves sexually pure in relating with others because this love will do only what honors God and honors the other individual (see Rom. 13:8-10).

Love Will Test Your Motives

The love test helps us to examine the motives of our heart. "Motive" is the reason behind what we do or say. By taking a moment to examine our reasons for doing what we plan to do, we can determine if they are pure or impure. The definition of pure is "cleanness; freedom from guilt or defilement of sin; having an innocence toward evil; free from mixture; being separated from the world's influence; free from moral defilement; freedom from contamination by illicit sexual connection; purity in language, chaste."[1]

In an excerpt from the book, *Every Man's Battle*, the authors paraphrase Hosea 8:5-6, saying, "What is going on here? Why are my children choosing to be impure? They are Christians, for heaven's sake! When are they going to start acting like it?"[2] We choose to walk pure or to allow impure thinking and behavior in our lives. It takes effort to resist impurity today because it seems to be all around us.

Purity is not being a mixture of God and the world.

Paul wrote to Timothy, "*Be an example (pattern) for the believers in speech, in conduct, in love, in faith, and in **purity***" (1 Tim. 4:12 AMP, emphasis added). Purity requires separating or making a difference between what is holy from that which is defiling.

When your motive is pure, you place a self-restraint on what you wear, what you say, where you go, and what you watch and listen to. Purity in motive affects everything in your life. When you walk in purity, your desire is to please God and not to cause others any difficulty in their relationship toward God.

A Christian girl with pure motives understands that the bra-less look doesn't encourage purity in the mind of a guy. Tight, see-through clothes challenge holy thinking in a guy's mind.

Paul wrote, "*Try instead to live in such a way that you will never make your brother stumble...*" (Rom. 14:13 TLB). Some Christians say, "That's too much bondage." However, my response is, "That's love."

Some girls feel that they should be free to wear whatever clothes they want to wear and that guys who have wrong thoughts because of it just have lust problems. *Your freedom in Jesus Christ does not mean you can do whatever you want to do. That's lust. Your freedom in Jesus Christ is based on doing whatever is motivated by love.* Galatians 5:13-14 says, "*You have been given freedom: not freedom to do wrong, but freedom to love and serve each other. For the whole Law can be summed up in this one command: 'Love others as you love yourself'*" (TLB). This kind of love is always aware of how what we do affects others.

Paul wrote in Romans 15:1-2:

Even if we believe that it makes no difference to the Lord whether we do these things, still we cannot just go ahead and do them to please ourselves; for we must bear the "burden" of being considerate of the doubts and fears of others—of those who feel these things are wrong. Let's please the other fellow, not ourselves, and do what is for his good and thus build him up in the Lord (TLB).

Love Accepts Responsibility for Others and Shows Self-Restraint

The love of God recognizes that what we do affects others— good or bad. We accept responsibility for others. We become aware that what we wear and what we do will be a help to a guy or a stumbling block in his Christian walk. This is being considerate or thoughtful.

I realize that in the Scripture, Paul had been talking about eating and drinking things that had been offered previously in idol worship, but his point was that whatever we do, we must evaluate our motives to see if we are being driven by our own selfishness, stubborn will, and lust or by the leading of the Holy Spirit and His love.

Galatians 5:16-17 says:

I advise you to obey only the Holy Spirit's instructions. He will tell you where to go and what to do, and then you won't always be doing the wrong things your evil nature wants you to. For we naturally love to do evil things that are just the opposite from the things that the Holy Spirit tells us to do; and the good things we want

to do when the Spirit has his way with us are just the opposite of our natural desires. These two forces within us are constantly fighting each other to win control over us, and our wishes are never free from their pressures (TLB).

Verses 19-23 say:

But when you follow your own wrong inclinations your lives will produce these evil results: impure thoughts, eagerness for lustful pleasure, idolatry, spiritism (that is, encouraging the activity of demons), hatred and fighting, jealousy and anger, constant effort to get the best for yourself, complaints and criticisms, the feeling that everyone else is wrong except those in your own little group—and there will be wrong doctrine, envy, murder, drunkenness, wild parties, and all that sort of thing. Let me tell you again as I have before, that anyone living that sort of life will not inherit the Kingdom of God. But when the Holy Spirit controls our lives he will produce this kind of fruit in us: love, joy, peace, patience, kindness, goodness, faithfulness, gentleness and self-control... (TLB).

The Holy Spirit will always lead us in the path or direction of love. *Love considers others besides themselves; lust does whatever it wants to do because lust justifies its freedom. Love seeks to help other people keep their focus on Jesus; lust seeks to attract and bring attention to oneself and will dress in whatever manner needed to bring attention to one's body.* The fashion world feeds on drawing attention to the body. This means that it feeds on creating lust. Stores everywhere sell clothes for the purpose of drawing attention to legs, breasts, belly buttons, and hips. Don't be afraid to dress with modest views. Your view toward modesty will reveal your love toward God and others.

Even though you have freedom, the love of God will develop a self-restraint within you that will guide you in what to wear and in how you come across to people. Like it or not, you are being watched by someone. Someone else is being guided by what they see in you.

First Corinthians 8:9 says, *"Be careful, however, that the exercise of your freedom does not become a stumbling block to the weak"* (NIV). Verse 12 goes on to say that when you sin against your brother and wound his weak conscience in this way, you are sinning against Christ.

How to Dress in a Way That Protects Others from Lusting After You

Some helpful thoughts are:

1. Buy a larger size than you normally would buy if you know the style is the "tight look." If you can't find a good fit that's modest, have an alteration person adjust it.

2. Look at yourself in the dressing room mirror when you try on a top and make sure it isn't revealing too much cleavage. Make sure it doesn't appear so tight that your bust is about to burst out of it and the buttons aren't being pulled apart as if they could pop open.

3. When buying pants, check that they aren't so tight on the buttocks and thighs that people can tell what kind of underwear you are wearing or when you slightly bend that your underwear (especially those who still wear thongs) shows. Also, ladies, if you have gained some weight and you are still trying to wear

those smaller sized pants, it could be embarrassing or even gross for others to look at you. Have mercy!

4. When wearing a skirt, make sure the length is not so short that when you barely bend over the top of your thighs and your underwear show. Those who may be required to stand on a high stage or walk up stairs need to be aware that higher heights mean legs and bottoms are in the face of those down below.

A strong and popular young Christian man who is a friend of ours from college was addressing a group of teenage girls at an event I attended. He shared from a guy's perspective of today's fashions and what Christian girls and women are wearing. He mentioned how difficult it has been for many young Christian men who want to walk godly. He ended his comments with this statement:

Some of you look like you get up in the morning and hang your small pants on a line, then jump into them because it looks like you've been poured into them. All I'm asking of you girls is to please show us guys some consideration and the love of God. Please don't wear clothes that would cause guys to stumble. We need you to dress more modestly.

He shared that girls who make the effort to dress more modestly actually love guys more than girls who dressed immodestly. One is based out of love and the other out of lust.

The God-kind of love (*agape*) does what will benefit others instead of themselves. God holds us responsible to consider the weaknesses of others. The love of God will always cause you to do the right thing.

"*If you love your neighbor* [anyone around your life] *as much as you love yourself you will not want to harm or cheat him....Love does no wrong to anyone. That's why it*

fully satisfies all of God's requirements..." (Rom. 13:9-10 TLB).
"Let love be your greatest aim..." (1 Cor. 14:1 TLB).

Take time to consider your ways and bring everything in your life to the feet of Jesus in surrender of your will to His.

Live by the law of love and in the spirit of surrender; people will then have no problem recognizing that you are a Christian.

Thoughts to Remember

Here are some closing thoughts to remember:

1. If we measure everything we do or say by the love test, we can determine whether or not we're being led by the Holy Spirit or by our own human lust. Love and lust are opposites.

2. The love test helps us to examine the motives of our heart. Motive is the reason behind what we do or say.

3. Purity of motives requires separating or making a difference between what is holy and what is defiling. Purity in your motives will affect everything in your life.

4. Love accepts responsibility for others. Love will not cause a brother to stumble. Love considers others besides themselves. Whereas, lust does whatever it wants to do and lust justifies its freedom. Love seeks to help other people keep their focus on Jesus; lust seeks to distract and bring attention to oneself in the way she dresses. The fashion world feeds on drawing attention to the body. You as a Christian have to understand the world's view and God's view.

5. Your view towards modesty will reveal your love toward God and others. The God-kind of love always does what honors God and will not cause others to stumble.

Endnotes

1. Noah Webster, *1828 American Dictionary of the English Language.*
2. Stephen Arterburn and Fred Stoeker, *Every Man's Battle* (Colorado Springs, CO: WaterBrook Press, 2000), 42.

OTHER BOOKS BY SHARON DAUGHERTY

Walking in the Fruit of the Spirit
Book (BS01) $9.00

Every Christian has been given the fullness of Jesus and the power of the Holy Spirit along with all of His fruit. Learn how to walk in the Spirit, deny the flesh, and live in the victory that Jesus has given to us. How are you going to walk it out?

Called By His Side
Book (BS02) $4.00

God sees a husband and wife as one flesh and one spirit. He doesn't call one-half of a spirit. He calls you as one. You don't have to be someone else but you have to be all that God has called you to be. Jesus needs every-one to walk out their purpose in this hour.

Avoiding Deception
Book (BS03) $10.00 Suggested retail price $13.99

Webster defines *deceived* as "when a person believes what is not truth to be truth...to be misled." How a Christian recognizes and responds to satan's tactics can determine his eternal destiny. If we are going to over-come to the end, we must guard our hearts from deception.

How Valuable Are Your Beliefs
(Valuable enough to stand for, live for and even die for?)
Mini book (BS05) $1.00

91% of this generation says there is no absolute truth. While public education and the media promote a message that there are no absolute moral values and that all values and beliefs are equal. Our country's moral foundation is slowly eroding away. Will you take a stand for what you believe and make a difference?

Pick up one of these great products by Sharon Daugherty. To order, call toll free at 1-888-874-8674, or visit us on the Web at www.victory.com.

Additional copies of this book and other book titles from DESTINY IMAGE are available at your local bookstore.

Call toll free: 1-800-722-6774.

Send a request for a catalog to:

Destiny Image® Publishers, Inc.

P.O. Box 310
Shippensburg, PA 17257-0310

"Speaking to the Purposes of God for this Generation and for the Generations to Come."

For a complete list of our titles, visit us at www.destinyimage.com